Somewhere in the Midlands

By the same authors

Letters For Victory - Brewin Books 1993

Somewhere
in the
Midlands

A History of U.S.A.A.F.
Station 522
Smethwick

Fran & Martin Collins

First published by Brewin Books Ltd.
Studley, Warwickshire

ISBN 1 85858 119 2

British Library Cataloguing in Publication Data

A Catalogue record for this book is available from The British Library

Typeset in Garamond Book
and made and printed in Great Britain by
Heron Press, Kings Norton, Birmingham

Contents

Foreword

"Behind these gigantic air assaults lies a story, not spectacular enough for headlines, but none the less essential - the story of supplies, and what particularly concerns us in this history, signal supplies. The roaring towmotors and bustling G.I.s weaving in and out of the long rows of stacked crates and boxes accounted for the very creditable_ _ _ shipping figures _ _, all the result of solid work days interrupted only by the one hour a day spent marching up to Guest Keen's Recreation Grounds* for a snappy drill session or other training activity."

Official History of Station 522

*Guest Keen and Nettlefolds Bolt and Nut Manufacturers on the corner of Norman Road and Thimble Road. This large industrial combine was one of the largest employers in Smethwick.

Introduction

On the 7th December 1941 the events at Pearl Harbor altered the United States position with regard to the war in Europe. Four days after Congress had declared war on Japan, Germany and Italy declared war on the United States. America found herself involved in a war on two fronts. This resulted in plans being made to send troops both to the Pacific and to the British Isles.

By the Spring of 1942 large numbers of American troops began arriving in the U.K. In order to prepare for the planned American air offensive against Germany a large scale airfield construction programme was undertaken to accommodate the fighter and bomber forces and their personnel. Many former R.A.F. stations were upgraded and transferred to the 8th and later 9th U.S,A.A,F.* In addition the U.S.A.A.F. administered a number of support installations such as Headquarters, Quartermaster depots and supply and maintenance depots.

The subject of this book is the main Air Force Signal Supply Depot which was located in Smethwick, a small industrial town in the Midlands, from the summer of 1943 until the end of the war. Its function was to store, supply, maintain and repair signal equipment used by the American airforces in England.

*In October 1943 the 9th Air Force made their base in England after a successful campaign in Europe.

Acknowledgments

In grateful acknowledgement of the following people and sources:

Edward Allen, Roland Andrews, Kathleen Bailey, John Blazek, Margaret Blazek, Allan L.Brown, Mr.Cartwright (formerly of Masons), Pamela Cashmore, Nora Crosbee, Jean Dean, Doyle L.Dillon, Margaret Doggett, Brian Gastinger, Charles G. Hinde, Peter Kennedy, Louis Kraft, Angela Maquire, Peggy Padfield, Margaret Parry, Mrs.Purslow, Ivy Royall, Vic Royall, Ada Thompson, Mr.B.Tomkins.

Bearwood Gazette

Official Guide to the Army Air Forces Pocket Book Inc.

Smethwick Local History Society.

Smethwick Telephone.

Spotlight Magazine.

Maxwell Air Force Base Archives Section for supplying the following unit histories:

History of 879th Signal Company Depot, Aviation.

History of 892nd Signal Company Depot, Aviation.

History of 908th Signal Company Depot, Aviation.

History of 21294th Q.M.Trucking Company.

History of U.S.A.A.F. Station 522.

Thanks are also due to Tim Jebbit for his photographic expertise.

Chapter One

The Birth of Station 522

The birth of Army Air Force Station 522, at Beakes Road, Smethwick, Staffordshire, England, took place on 25th August 1943 in order to meet the increasing demands of the United States Army Air Forces in the European Theatre of Operations. By the Summer of 1943 the U.S.A.A.F had established itself in Britain and had grown considerably from the first contingent of seven officers who flew to the United Kingdom by Dakota in February 1942.

Situated at least fifty miles from the nearest U.S. Air Force base, Smethwick would seem an unlikely site for an air force supply depot but, in fact, a midlands location was ideal for the movement, of equipment throughout the country. Another factor in Smethwick's favour was the unlikeliness of the location. Its distance from the airfields it served gave the depot a degree of security. John Blazek, a former G.I. from the base suggests that:

"We were stationed at Beakes Road to be as small and unnoticed as possible from the enemy."

The Station at Beakes Road and the subdepot at Leicester (A.A.F. 527) were to be part of a network of stations in the Base Air Depot Area commanded by Colonel Ott from the Headquarters at Burtonwood (B.A.D. 1) in Lancashire.* To maintain an efficient operation in obtaining signal supplies and equipping the station with the necessary transportation to deliver the supplies it was essential to maintain cooperation between Colonel Ott, Colonel Dixon (Signal Officer of the 8th Air Force), Lieutenant Colonel Custer (Signal Officer of the Base Air Depot Area) and Major Leslie C.Heartz, the Depot Commander for Station 522.

The depot at Smethwick was to be initially manned by the 908th Signal Depot Company, Aviation, This company had been activated on 25th July 1942 at Burtonwood Air Depot. The original personnel of the group came from the 751st Signal Platoon which was based at Burtonwood. A number of these men had been involved in communication work in civilian life prior to joining the armed forces. (Several of the personnel had worked for the well known Bell Telephone Company.) On 3rd September the 756th Signal Platoon, consisting of four officers and 69 enlisted men, under the command of Captain Leslie C. Heartz, were transferred into the 908th.

At this point Captain Heartz had already had a long and distinguished career in the U.S. Forces. He had first seen service in the First World War as a radioman with the U.S. Navy. He was released from active duty in 1922 and entered the employ of

* See Appendix 2.

1

Beakes Road 1934. Worlds Wear Factory on left
(Smethwick Local Studies Archives)

the New England Telephone and Telegraph Company at Boston, Massachusetts, Five years later he was commissioned a 2nd Lieutenant in the Signal Corps Officers Reserve Corps where he served as a Radio Aide to the Commanding Officer of the 1st Corps Area, He then moved to Maine where he joined the National Guard and was commissioned a 1st Lieutenant of the Field Artillery in 1931. In 1937 he was promoted to Captain and assumed command of Regimental Headquarters Battery. Following the events at Pearl Harbor Heartz was called to active duty with the 43rd Division and after completing manouveres in Louisiana and field artillery training at Fort Sill, Oklahoma he was transferred to the Signal Corps. In June 1942 he was assigned to the '7th Air Depot Group where he served as Executive Officer. Heartz travelled overseas to the U.K. in August 1942.

August was also the month that the 908th were moved to Poynton Advance Depot in Cheshire. In September Higher Headquarters directed that the 908th should be transferred into the 12th Air Force, therefore preparations were made to move the company overseas to the Mediterranean Theatre of Operations, but before the orders could be carried out they were rescinded and it was decided that the company should remain as a part of the 8th Air Force. At this point the 908th was one of only two Signal Aviation Companies assigned to the European Theatre of Operations and therefore the equipment and skills of the group were in great demand. It was the 908th's duty to supply the entire 8th Air Force with signal equipment. The unit were also responsible for furnishing telephone and teletype operators; message centre clerks; couriers; construction, installation and repair crews; radio operators and maintenance personnel to both R.A.F. and U.S.A.A.F. depots operational throughout the U.K (including Wales and Ireland).

"On the 4th December 1942 the company almost had its first casualty in the U.S. Invasion of England when Lt. Pearce, returning to N. Ireland in an Oxford twin engine training plane after a visit to Burtonwood Air Depot, crashed in the Welsh hills near Sealand. Lt. Pearce and his pilot were not seriously injured and Lt. Pearce returned to duty on 16th December 1942."*

December also saw the promotion of Captain Heartz to Major and Higher Headquarters began to look for a larger site for the Signal Depot as the available space at Poynton was becoming inadequate. Fourteen Iris Hut warehouses in Sudbury, Derbyshire, were chosen for the new location and Major Heartz was made commander of the new station (A.A.F. Station 158). which became the Main Air Force Signal Supply Depot.

By the summer of 1943 storage space for air force signal equipment in Britain was rapidly reaching a saturation point. Due to this factor and the increased demand for signal equipment from Strategic and Tactical Air Depots in the United Kingdom# it became necessary for Higher Headquarters to find a more suitable location. After an intensive search and lengthy negotiations an available site was located in Smethwick, Staffordshire.

On 25th August 1943 the Headquarters and Shipping and Records Sections, which consisted of five officers and 67 enlisted men were moved to Smethwick to prepare the new location for operation. Detachment A, consisting of three officers and 96 enlisted men remained at Station 158.

Prior to its acquisition by the U.S.A.A.F. the building at Smethwick had served as a textile manufacturing plant and was known as the 'Worldswear Pinafore Factory'. Upon the factory's requisition it was necessary for army personnel to dismantle all the machinery in the building and prepare it for storage and transfer.

When the men from Sudbury arrived to complete the job, Peggy Padfield, a former employee of Worldswear, recalls being amazed at the speed they worked to move all the equipment. She remembers that it only took them a weekend, Peggy was one of the few remaining staff that went in to 'tidy up' the following weekend. She also remembers that the Americans were not allowed to 'fraternise' with the factory staff. She recalls that the factory employees would sit at one end of the canteen while the G.I.s used the other.

"They used to file in clutching their mugs, plates etc. and queue to be served. They seemed to have plenty of food. One day Top Sergeant Tracey walked the length of the canteen to present me with half a tin of sliced peaches, amid loud whistles and cheers. I'm sure I blushed from my head to my toes! Of course with our wartime rations a half tin of peaches was a real treat!"

*History of 908th Signal Company.
#See Appendix 2.

Beakes Road Factory 1994. (M. Collins)

Once the factory was empty it was necessary to make certain modifications to the building to adapt it for handling signal supplies. It was necessary to construct a second floor capable of carrying the weight of power machinery, modify a number of entrances to permit the loading and unloading of supplies and provide office accommodation for both the officers and the enlisted men.

Although the Americans made extensive alterations to the factory they were able to utilise some of the existing facilities. Peggy Padfield remembers them discovering the chute at the top end of the factory by which small cartons of packed clothes had been sent down to the basement for packing into wooden crates:

"One day I was with my boss in the basement talking to an American officer, when suddenly, descending headfirst down this chute came a delighted American dressed in 'fatigues' with his cap on back to front. The smile was certainly wiped from his face when he landed in a heap in view of his officer."

By the end of the year it was decided that the job of storage and supply was too big for one unit, therefore on 30th December 1943 the personnel and equipment of the 1061st Signal Company Service Group were transferred to the 908th Company to bring the organisational strength up to the authorised strength.

Although it was soon working at authorised strength the company still found it difficult to keep up with demands so another unit was sent to Station 522 to work alongside the 908th. On the 17th January 1944 the 892nd Signal Depot Company, Aviation was assigned to Smethwick.

This company had been activated in February 1943 at Pocono Mountains Military Reservation and Artillery Target Range in Tobyhanna, Pennsylvania. From Tobyhanna the company moved to Syracuse, New York and then to New Orleans in Louisiana before travelling to Camp Myles, Standish in Massachusetts which would be its Port of Embarkation. In December 1943 the company boarded the 'George V. Goethals' (referred to as B.O. 450 for security reasons) in Boston Harbour. As the company historian recorded the moment:

*"The 892nd was off for their first nautical adventure to a spam eating army"**

After crossing the Atlantic Ocean the ship sailed up the Firth of Clyde and the company disembarked at Glasgow. From here they travelled by train to Dinton in Wiltshire where they were billeted in pyramidal tents. At the beginning of 1944 the 892nd was transferred from the 9th to the 8th Air Force and sent to Station 522 where they were consolidated with the 908th in running the operations of the station under the command of Major Heartz. At this point the historian for the 892nd commented:

*"Noteworthy is the fact that the living conditions here were an improvement beyond the expectations of most of the men. They were billeted in evacuated English homes with sufficient provisions for sanitation and heat.**

*History of the 892nd Company.

Side views of building with author's jeep. (M. Collins)

*Members of the 908th Signal Depot Company Aviation
at Station 522. (K. Bailey)*

6

One of the new company's first assignments was to consign Detachment A, consisting of two officers and 28 enlisted men to carry out the work of the subdepot at Leicester. Although the subdepot had been placed under the command of Station 522 in October 1943 the building was still occupied by a British cabinet company. It took three weeks for the men to move the company out and transform the building into a signal supply warehouse. Detachment B of the 892nd, consisting of one officer and 85 enlisted men was assigned to Burtonwood Air Depot as teletype and telephone operators, radio and radar maintenance men, code clerks and message centre clerks,

Because the two companies were working in close cooperation it was necessary to make some changes in the rosters of the officers at Station 522. This was particularly the case in the first few months of 1944 when the station underwent a number of administrative changes. This is how the roster of the two companies at Station 522 stood by the end of March 1944, noting changes occurring previous to this date:

908th Signal Depot Company, Aviation.

Name.	Duty
Maj. Leslie C. Heartz	Commanding Officer.
1st Lt. Granville H. Coleman.	Company Commander, (Formerly Station Adjutant and Personnel Officer.)
1st Lt. Clyde G. Underwood.	Signal Supply Officer.
lst. Lt. Albert H. Heath	Assistant Signal Supply Officer.
1st Lt. John H. Pratel	Station Communications Officer.
1st Lt. Walter A. Bachus.	Commanding Officer, Detachment A at Station 158. (Formerly assigned Station Commander at station 527.)
2nd Lt. Horace V. Pfeiffer	General Repair Officer.
2nd Lt. Raymond W. Shaddy	Depot Property Officer.
W. O. J. G. Robert E. Thiery	Station Adjutant and Personnel Officer.
W.O.J.G. Oliver F Sundsmo.	Assistant General Repair Officer. (Originally assigned to the 892nd.)
W.O.J.G. Orlo B. Elfes.	Assistant Signal Supply Officer at A.A.F. 158
Lt. Smith	Transferred at beginning of 1944 to H.Q. 9th Air Service Command.
Lt. Duerr.	Transferred at beginning of 1944 to 9th Fighter Command.

Members of 892nd Company at BAD1, Burtonwood. (N. Crosbee)

892nd Signal Company Depot, Aviation.

Name	Duty.
Capt.James B. Holly	Station Executive Officer (Formerly Company Commander of 908th.)
1st Lt.Rudolph F. Keyworth	Company Commander and Summary Court Officer.
1st Lt.Jack L. Echelson	Commanding Officer Detachment B at Station 590.
2nd Lt.Robert B.Cochran	Station Commander at Subdepot A.A.F. 527 from March 1944. (Formerly Commanding Officer of Detachment A., 892nd at A.A.F. 527.)
2nd Lt.Leon D.Epstein	Motor Transport Officer.
2nd Lt.Louis J.Wohlgemuth.	Assistant Signal Supply Officer. (Transferred from 908th.)
2nd Lt.Howard E.Church.	Plant Protection Officer. (Transferred from 908th.)
2nd Lt.Robert B.Lucas.	Station Education Officer.
C.P.O.Felix G.Sorrentino.	Commanding Officer, Detachment A, 892nd at A.A.F. 527 from March 1944.
C.P.O.Beryl C.Zumwalt	Instructor for 9th Air Force American Radio and Cryptographic School at Kidderminster.
W.0.J.G. Jacob G.P.Rabinowitz.	Radio Maintenance at A.A.F. 590, Detachment B.
W.O.J.G.Vinifred R,Schell	Message Centre Officer at A.A.F. 586. (Transferred from 908th.)
Lt.Mervin Rubin	Released from duty with 892nd and assigned to A.S.C. U.S.S.T.A.F. in March 1944.

In March 1944 the depot was redesignated the Main Air Force Signal Supply Depot and both the 908th and the 892nd were transferred from assignment with the 8th Air Force Service Command to the United States Strategic Tactical Air Forces in Europe, under the command of Lt.General Spaatz.

Chapter Two

Progress, Efficiency and High Morale.

The personnel of Station 522 were divided into ten distinct sections. Each section had a role to play in the efficient running of the station. The principal seven sections were:

1.   Headquarters Section.

2.   Storage and Issue Section.

3.   Depot Property Section.

4.   Transportation Section.

5.   Communications Section.

6.   General Repair Section.

7.   Plant Protection Section.

The above sections carried out the main duties of the depot. Three other sections existed, they were:

8.   Medical Section.

9.   Special Service Section.

10.   Education Section.

I. HEADQUARTERS SECTION.
This section was headed by Major Heartz and dealt with the administration and coordination of the other sections.

2. STORAGE AND ISSUE SECTION.
The main function of Station 522 was to receive, store and issue signal supplies for the United States Army Air Force, The Storage and Issue Section took up the major part of the floor space in the factory building to store signal supplies and equipment peculiar to the air force. This category included such items as radios and radio parts, 'chaff'* and other communication equipment.
The section was headed by the Signal Supply Officer, Lt. Underwood (known by

* Used by Allied planes to scramble radar

Eddie Allen at his desk in Major Heartz's office. (K. Bailey)

G.I.s outside station 522.
(K. Bailey)

the enlisted men as 'Underdrawers') and the Assistant Signal Supply Officers. The section consisted of three subsections, The first subsection dealt with storage and consisted of 30 enlisted men whose duties were to receive all stock entering the depot and to store it for reshipping. Much of the equipment came directly from the United States.

The second subsection dealt with shipping and consisted of 18 enlisted men whose duties were to fill the requisitions from stock and pack the stock ready for delivery. Packing tables ran the length of the warehouse to enable the men to carry out their duties. Two towmotor cars were available for the subsection to move the heavy packing cases.

The third subsection dealt with stock control and consisted of eight enlisted men under the supervision of the chief clerk and the chief Stock Control Clerk. This group carried out all posting and filing of requisitions that arrived at the station. A filing and record system was established that:

"enabled it to obtain a complete history of any particular item at a moment's notice."#

The chief clerk of this section had a cartoon prominently displayed on the door of his office:
"Under the picture of the infamous paperhanger* being nailed into a wooden crate is written:

'Your job has no glamour no doubt
-And your chances for fame are slim.
But what are you crying about?
Just look what you're doing to him!'"#

The remaining personnel of the Storage and Issue Section formed a link between the three subsections.

Requisitions for the equipment stored at Smethwick came from the four Strategic Air Depots (8th Air Force), the six Tactical Air Depots[+] (9th Air Force) and any other unit that was authorised to deal directly with the Main Air Force Signal Supply Depot.

Requisitions came in by telephone, teletype and letter and were directed to the Supply Officer who examined them and forwarded them to the Stock Control Subsection, This subsection edited the requisitions, noted priorities, determined availability of and entered the issue approved quantities in the stock records. The requisitions were then registered, given shipping tickets and delivered to the Shipping Subsection.

*Hitler had been a decorator in civilian life.
#History of Station 522
+See Appendix 2.

For requisitions which could not be filled due to stock shortages, a note was made and sent to the supply officer who forwarded the list to H.Q.,8th A.A.F. Service Command. The lists would then be forwarded to the appropriate source, either S.O.S. in Britain, A.S.C. in the United States or the British Air Ministry. The forthcoming stock would be shipped to the Receiving Subdepot at Sudbury or the Bulk Storage Subdepot at Leicester. Eventually it would arrive at the warehouse in Beakes Road to continue the distribution process.

3. DEPOT PROPERTY SECTION

This section consisted of one officer and ten enlisted men who had been assigned to the Quartermaster Section at Sudbury previous to their assignment to Smethwick. The section were responsible for procuring and upkeeping the living and working quarters of the unit. The Post Exchange (P.X.)* came under the jurisdiction of this section. Two men were employed here to make out requisitions, keep records and pick up Post Exchange supplies for the depot.

4. TRANSPORTATION SECTION

Initially only three men (two drivers and a dispatcher) were sent to Smethwick from Sudbury to handle transportation for the depot. As a result of the increase in demand for the delivery of signal supplies it was soon necessary to Increase the number of vehicles and drivers, In a short time the motor pool increased its staff to 22 drivers and three dispatchers. Drivers were assigned their own vehicles and were expected to make two or three 200 mile trips per week. 2nd Lt.Epstein was assigned as Transportation Officer and Sgt.Theodore Berg of the 892nd was given supervision of the Motor Pool.

The mechanics at the base were able to carry out first and second echelon maintenance work on the company's vehicles. First echelon maintenance required daily inspection, servicing and fuelling vehicles and carrying out minor repairs. Second echelon maintenance involved periodic preventative inspections and such adjustments, repairs and replacements as may be accomplished with hand tools and mobile equipment. This included tasks such as checking timing, adjusting valves and changing engines.

The Ordnance Subsection came into being in May 1944 and was affiliated to the Transportation Section. Through this subsection Lt.Epstein was able to centralise the control of the two company armourers and the machinist working with the machine shop truck. The armourer's s job was to prepare weapons for turning in and to receive new ones.

5. COMMUNICATIONS SECTION.

The Communications Section consisted of five subsections. The first subsection,

*Post Exchange - equivalent to British NAAFI.

the Message Center,"nerve centre of Station 522",* commenced operations on the opening of the station, This subsection which was composed of a message center chief and two assistants, handled all incoming and outgoing teletype messages, all mail and the shipping of special packages. A pick up of outgoing mail from each office was scheduled for every half hour during operation hours. This subsection was also responsible for distributing special circulars and papers to each office.

The personnel of the Teletype Subsection had spent some time working with the teletype sections of both the R.A.F. (British) and the S.O.S. (American), prior to them being assigned to the depot at Smethwick. They had been detached to the R.A.F. stations that were being converted to A.A.F. stations to organise and operate until permanent signal companies could be assigned to the stations. While carrying out this type of work a complete knowledge of operating procedures of both air forces was gained.

The Cryptographic Subsection worked in the 'Code Room' and was composed of one officer and four enlisted men who had been trained at the British Cryptographic School, The Code Room contained the equipment and facilities required for the coding, decoding, encyphering and decyphering of messages in the European Theatre of Operations. Prior to the opening of the Code Room at Station 522 cryptographic message were processed at a nearby Allied Station.

The Telephone Subsection operated the switchboards for both station 522 and Station 158. Initially the men used the pinafore factory's existing telephone switchboard. Operations were commenced with five telephone operators and one chief operator. By the end of 1943 there were seven telephone operators. One of the factory's former office staff, Peggy Padfield, was retained at the depot for a short time in August 1943 to instruct the Americans in the use of the telephone system. She recalls:

"The telephone system was the type where there were about three outside lines and several extensions which were operated by key type plugs. The telephone box had a handle at the side which one turned to ring through to an extension. Very simple really, but maybe a bit confusing to an American."

Peggy also remembers the handsome top sergeant that worked with her in the office:

"He was the exact double of Clark Gable, and you can imagine how I felt as a young impressionable girl of 15 and crazy about Clark Gable, when he appeared in the office doorway and spoke to me in a soft southern drawl. In his American uniform, peaked cap tilted slightly, slow smile, soft voice, American accent, he sure made an impression on me."

*History of Station 522.

Station 158, Sudbury, Derbyshire.

Allan Linwood Brown with Jeep and mess tin. (K. Bailey)

The Communications Section also had a subsection that was responsible for the installation and maintenance of wire lines of communication. This subsection had the use of a construction vehicle complete with all facilities for pole line construction and field work. The personnel working for this subsection included installers, repairmen, construction linemen, switchboard installers and switchboard maintenance men.

The erection of the flagpole on the base was carried out by this section. Kathleen Bailey (nee Thompson) remembers that a large Stars and Stripes flag, which was ten foot by 19 foot, was flown every day in fair weather. It was hoisted at reveille and taken down at dusk, In bad weather a smaller 'storm flag', which was five foot by nine foot was flown.

The Communications Section also provided the fire defence team for the station.

6. GENERAL REPAIR SECTION

This section was commanded by Lt.Pfeiffer until May 1944 when he left on indefinite Temporary Duty and was replaced by C. W. 0. Zumwalt. The section consisted of two officers and 15 enlisted men.

The Shop Subsection of this section was located in the basement of the depot where large benches had been constructed for electronic servicing. Master Sergeant Getshaw oversaw the men in this shop. It carried out all the machine shop work for the station and installed all the wiring jobs on the station premises. It was also responsible for the charge and maintenance of all fire extinguishers. Shop tools and spare parts for typewriters and automotive equipment were carried in stock.

Tech.4 Louis Kraft, a member of this sub section, recalls the time when he was asked to design a tester for the quartz crystals handled by the depot. The Headquarters of the 8th Air Force had sent orders that the depot should improve the handling and distribution of the quartz crystals that passed through Station 522. These particular crystals had a widespread use as they were fitted in SCR/522 receivers which were carried in all planes flown by the U.S.A.A.F. and the R.A.F. Apparently many of the air bases were receiving defective crystals. Louis attributes this to rough handling during loading and unloading, as they were very fragile. Louis had worked as a fixture builder in civilian life and therefore had had experience of building test sets, so Master Sergeant Guetchaw asked him to design and build some crystal testers to test the crystals in the depot. A couple of days later the Master Sergeant approached Louis to ask if he could modify the tester so that the crystals could be tested while still in their boxes so that time could be saved. Louis was able to do this and the job of testing the 67,800 crystals was completed in two weeks instead of the two months that Headquarters had allowed for the task. Louis remembers that neither he or the other sergeant working on this project:

"got any increase in rank or any recognition from any of our officers at all for this really remarkable piece of work."

The Radio Subsection of this section carried out all the repair work of the Signal Corps ground and air force radio and radar equipment. Station 522 was responsible for carrying out third and fourth echelon maintenance on the radio and radar equipment in the Base Air Depot Area. Third echelon maintenance consisted of repairs and replacements requiring mobile machinery and equipment which could be transported by road to the bases where needed. This could involve field repairs, salvage, removal and replacement of major unit assemblies, fabrication of minor parts and minor repairs. Normally third echelon repairs could be completed in a limited time. On the other hand fourth echelon maintenance consisted of complete restoration or repair of equipment, fabrication of parts that were required to supplement the normal supply, technical modifications and salvaging useful equipment.

The General Repair Section was also engaged in the work of station gas defence and was responsible for the upkeep and repair of damaged gas sets.

7. PLANT PROTECTION SECTION.

This section consisted of one officer of the guard, two sergeants of the guard and 16 guards who worked on a two shift system around the clock. They were responsible for protecting the property of the station and the station itself. The guards checked that all incoming and outgoing vehicles had the necessary trip tickets. They were also responsible for seeing that only authorised personnel were allowed on the base.

Stationary and roving guards were armed with semi-automatic weapons. Kathleen Bailey remembers asking a guard called Eddie if he ever got bored on guard duty. His reply was that he would rather be pulling the trigger of his gun on active duty.

8. MEDICAL SECTION

In April 1944 Captain Christian G. Ward (attached to 908th Company) arrived at the depot from 311th Dispensary to take up the post of Depot Medical Officer. His arrival eliminated the need for daily trips off base for the men on sick call and ensured that the men did not need to be absent from their duties for any great length of time. In September Captain Ward was relieved of attachment to the 908th but remained at the station to look after the welfare of the men. A dispensary and an ambulance (which acted as a temporary first aid post) were added to the department to help it run more efficiently.

9. SPECIAL SERVICE SECTION.

This section consisted of three enlisted men and W.O.J.G. Washburn. Its function was to ensure that both the morale of the unit and public relations were kept at a high level. The Special Service supervised the extra curricular activities of the men, It arrived at the base in August 1943 and its first task was to procure a set of horseshoes, a baseball bat, a baseball and gloves. Games of baseball and horseshoes were organised in the yard outside the depot.

Once the living quarters for the soldiers had been established this section furnished a dayroom with games, radio, record player, tables and chairs. The section also conducted its own War Bond drives, encouraging the men of the unit to purchase bonds by printing posters and displaying them about the station, One of the posters was to be found in the Motor Pool Office. It read:

"IMMEDIATE ATTENTION

Subject: Secret Mission.

To: You Soldier.

Sir:

1. You are my Commanding Officer. Your signature will release me for active combat immediately.
2. I will take a crack at Schicklegruber and Tojo for you personally.
3. You will not have to sacrifice greatly to employ me.
4. I will do my share to keep the prices down, both for your folks at home, and for you while you're over here.
5. You can recall me any time after 60 days.
6. But if you allow me to complete my 10 year mission I will return to you 4% greater in substance and value, and I will help you to buy a home, help educate your family or aid you to do what you want most at that time.
7. If you choose to ignore this request no one will ever know but you will never forget.
    Please send me at once.
    Respectfully
    Private U.S.Bond."*

Other noteworthy projects attended to by the Special Service Section were: attending to the shopping needs of the personnel; acquisition of a film projector, enabling the men to have motion picture facilities on the station; helping to plan furloughs for the enlisted men and sponsoring company parties. This section also worked alongside the civilian population of the local area, supplying and producing musical entertainment for civilian functions,

A further responsibility of this section was the setting up of a library, In the first few months of 1944 the library consisted of around 60 books and 150 magazines.

*History of Station 522.

Magazines available in the Special Service Library.

The range of magazines included:
Esquire, Life, Time, Newsweek, Coronet, Colliers, Popular Mechanics and various comics.

The base did not have a permanent chaplain but Protestant and Catholic chaplains visited the station on alternate weeks, One wonders if they saw the poster outside the Special Service Section which read:

"Special Service - For Your Pleasure;
Try us first, then the chaplain, if you must,"*

The Special Service did procure a pump organ and hymnals for the use of the chaplains at the noontime service held every Sunday.

10. EDUCATION SECTION.

The Education Officer, Lt.Lucas, was responsible for conducting 'Army Talks' (educational and propaganda talks produced by the U.S. Army Information and Education Division.) It was intended that these would take the form of informal discussions based upon the content of a weekly publication sent to all of the American bases through the Special Service. Army Talks were designed to:

* History of Station 522.

"aid personnel to become better informed men, to stimulate their thoughts and discussion and to listen to opinions offered by associates."*

but Lt.Lucas did encounter problems when:

"attempting to arouse the enlisted men's interest in the topics chosen for discussion."*

Nine classes were taken each week, although the average attendance was only 35 enlisted men per class.

In addition to 'Army Talks' the Education Service aimed to promote the correspondence course that were offered in the European Theatre of Operations. A number of Universities in the States had made it possible for the soldiers to continue study towards a degree while in the service through taking correspondence courses. Lt.Lucas also made it possible for the men to attend evening classes available in the local vicinity free of charge.

It appears that, at least at first, the Education service was not able to encourage as many men as it would have liked to take up the several sources of Education offered. As the official records state:

"It is desired that the future will see still further growth and greater advantages offered by this section."*

The Station Historian concludes his report of the sections:

"Thus went the life and work of Station 522 - - - it is a story of progress, efficiency and high morale."*

* History of Station 522.

CHART SHOWING FLOW OF SUPPLY

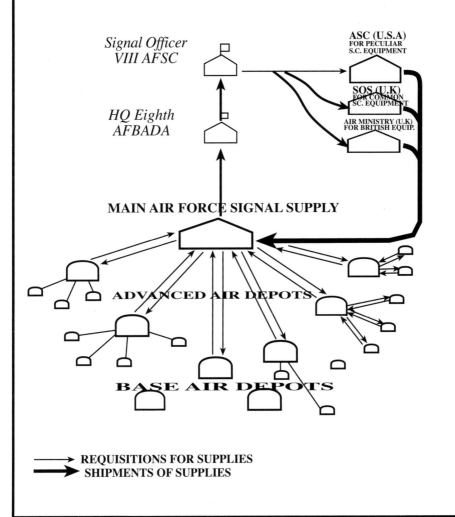

Signal Officer
VIII AFSC

ASC (U.S.A)
FOR PECULIAR
S.C. EQUIPMENT

SOS (U.K)
FOR COMMON
SC. EQUIPMENT

AIR MINISTRY (U.K)
FOR BRITISH EQUIP.

HQ Eighth
AFBADA

MAIN AIR FORCE SIGNAL SUPPLY

ADVANCED AIR DEPOTS

BASE AIR DEPOTS

REQUISITIONS FOR SUPPLIES
SHIPMENTS OF SUPPLIES

Chapter Three

Maximum Efficiency. August 1943 - May 1944

*"The current history of Station 522 and subordinate units - - - is factual evidence of the increased tempo and the enormous proportions that this war has assumed. The constant flow of supplies through this Depot is evidence of the strength of our nation and the determination our purpose."**

- so the unit historian introduces his records for the first few months of 1944.

H.Q. Section

Between January and March 1944 there were:

*"-some exchanges of personnel to bring the rosters of both companies to close compliance with the tables of organisation."**

(See Chapter 2. for details of transfers and changes in officer's duties for the two signal companies.) Also during the early part of 1944 the 951st Signal Radio Intelligence Company was attached to the 908th for administrative purposes. This company, commanded by William C.Brinson was located forty miles away from the base and was composed of seven assigned officers, 207 assigned enlisted men and 53 attached enlisted men..

In April 1944 the normal working pattern was altered to cope with the increased workload at the base. An extra half hour was added both at the start and end of the day. In addition to the duties that each section was involved in the men were expected to spend one hour per day at drill practice. Jean Dean remembers passing the soldiers drilling on her way to and from Uplands School. She recalls that the men would spend lunchtimes at drill in Thimblemill Road. Because of the absence of traffic (due to petrol rationing) the stretch of road between Addebrooke Road and the island at the bottom of Thimblemill Road could be used like a barracks square. Vic Royall remembers that the men also used to march to the Avery Sports Ground, on the Hagley Road, to drill although he does remark that he had never seen such awful marching in his life!

In May Major Heartz was relieved of duty and assignment with the 908th and assigned to H.Q., B.A.D.A., A.S.C, U.S.S.T.A.F., A.A.F. 590 (Burtonwood), He remained attached to the 908th and continued his duties as Station Commander of Station 552. During this time 1st Lt.Coleman was given the extra responsibility of

* History of Station 522.

Depot Commander along with his duties of Station Communications, Intelligence Officer and Assistant Top Secret Control Officer. In June Heartz was released from attachment to the 908th and attached to the 892nd.

Storage and Issue Section.

The total poundage of shipping handled by the base increased as the months went by. In January 1944 the base handled 40,000 pounds, February's figures were over 600,000 pounds while March's figures exceeded 5,000,000 pounds. In one week of March alone (17th-23rd) 2,639,955 pounds were handled. All this was achieved with no increase in personnel or equipment. Frequently the men of this section had to work on a 24 hour basis to ensure prompt delivery to the units needing the supplies.

The reason for the increase in the amount of supplies handled was that the depot was affected by an administrative change from above during March. As the official records state:

*"The redesignation of various higher headquarters resulted in an extension of the Depot's activities to the service of signal supplies for other air forces beside the Eighth. Naturally the demands of these other (air) forces required a tremendous increase in shipping."**

In April the station had been instructed to cease handling specialist items other than for the Eighth Air Force. The Ninth was able to obtain items common to both air forces through Station 522, although materials peculiar to itself had to be acquired through other means. In May there was yet another administrative change and from this month only the units under the command of B.A.D.A., A.S.C. and U.S.S.T.A.F. were to be allowed to requisition common signal supplies from the Smethwick Depot. Strategic Air Depots servicing the Ninth Air Force were to requisition supplies through the Air Service Command.

During May 1944 Lt.Heath took over the duties of Signal Supply Officer for the depot, replacing Lt. Underwood, who assumed command of the 908th Company. Also in May A.A.F. 802 (Baverstock), which was formerly a Ninth Air Force H.Q. Base Depot, became an intransit depot for Station 522.

Depot Property Section

The first priority of this section in August 1943 was to submit requisitions to the R.A.F. Liason Officer for such items as beds and bedding for the use of the men stationed there. The section also obtained contracts for laundry (The Criterion Laundry, now the Sunlight Laundry in Beakes Road, was used.), dry cleaning and shoe and clothing repair. All bills for the above services were signed at the Depot Property Section and forwarded to the Base Quartermaster for payment.

*History of Station 522.

Houses in Melville Road 1995. (M. Collins)
Formerly enlisted men's quarters

The Depot Property Section undertook to improve conditions at the depot by carrying out the following:

a. Erecting seven nissen huts, one for food storage, two to use as a motor pool garage, two for use as company orderly rooms and two for use as offices for the companies on the post.

b. Resurfacing the motor pool and driveway outside the mess hall.

c. Converting the basement of the depot into offices for the Armourer, Depot Property section, Post Exchange, Barber, Dispensary, Special Service and the mail clerk. An electrician's workshop was constructed In the boiler room.

d. Erecting an officers mess, a message centre with a wall for telephone charging units, a guard booth, a storehouse for paint and fire equipment and a shipping platform.

e. Installing lighting upstairs and in the basement of the depot.

f. Obtaining blackout curtains from the R.A.F. for use at the depot and in the living quarters.

g. Constructing offices for the Communications Officer and Officer of the Day.

h. Building a storage battery room for General Repair and a shop complete with workbench for the use of the Utilities Repair.

i. Reconditioning an Air Raid shelter for use as headquarters of the Plant Protection Officer, rewiring it and also rewiring the tented area.

In 1944 the Depot Property section took over the running of the enlisted men's mess hall. An extension was erected and an outside cement garbage pit was built. Other renovations were carried out as was recorded:

*"Hardworking, hungry G.I.s have been pleased to find their eating place sparkling with a fresh coat of paint, a renovated serving counter, neat racks and shelves built for holding culinary equipment and supplies."**

Aswell as the extensive building, repair and renovation that this section was responsible for the personnel made use of the artists in the unit to produce challenging posters to position around the depot. They carried such messages as:

"THIS IS A WAR OF SUPPLY
SIGNAL SUPPLY IS AS VITAL AS BLOOD PLASMA"*

and

"ZIP YOUR LIP
SILENCE IS A SECRET WEAPON"*

The Depot Property section was also responsible for acquiring living quarters for the men. It was necessary to submit requests for the requisition of buildings to the District Engineer, Central Midlands District, The section submitted a request to the District Engineer for several large houses for use as the men's living quarters. They also requested the use of two 500 gallon capacity petrol pumps located in

* History of Station 522.

28

379, Hagley Road 1995, formely Officers' Quarters. (M. Collins)

202, Hagley Road 1995, formely quarters of 892nd Company. (M. Collins)

Thimblemill Road and known as Thimblemill Garage. This request was granted at the beginning of November 1943. At the time the garage consisted of two pumps and an old shack. The Plant Protection Section was responsible for guarding the petrol pumps as petrol was a valuable commodity during wartime, It was necessary to requisition petrol for the depot's vehicles from the R.A.F.

The engineer also gave permission for the requisition of two houses in Hagley Road. One of them (number 431) still stands but the other (317) has since been demolished. The Depot Property Section had the houses cleaned and supplied with the necessary equipment and the men were able to move into their billets at the end of September 1943. John Blazek was billeted in number 317. He remembers that he shared a downstairs room with eight other men from his section. The two houses stood between one and two miles from the depot at Beakes Road and usually a truck would come to pick up the men when they were due to go on duty although occasionally the G.I.s would cycle the short distance.

In November permission was given for two houses in Melville Road to be used as additional living quarters. It was necessary to build additional latrines here and at the houses in Hagley Road. On the 23rd March 1944 number 379, Hagley Road (which is now part of the Woodlands Hotel) was handed over for use as officer's quarters while in May arrangements were made for 202, Hagley Road (now used as offices) to be used as living quarters for the enlisted men. of the 892nd Company, thereby bringing the company together under one roof. Two further houses were requisitioned for use as living quarters: 127, Hagley Road (since demolished to make way for modern houses) and 127, Portland Road.

The move into houses was welcomed by the men as prior to this their homes were large bell tents pitched in the land adjacent to the depot on the Reginald Road side. Jean Dean remembers passing them as she walked home from the Windsor Cinema. On cold, wintry nights the wind would blow the bottom flaps of the tents up, exposing the men's feet to the elements. She reflects:

"You could not help feeling sorry for them,"

The Station Historian's notes on the work of the Depot Property Section read as follows:

*"The men of this section have shown themselves fine carpenters, painters and plumbers and all round handymen."**

and

*"The exterior aspect of this station is in a continuous state of improvement as a result of the activities of the Depot Property Section, "**

* History of Station 522.

Transportation Section

As a result of an increase in the number of vehicles being dispatched it was necessary to man the motor pool on a 24 hour basis during the early part of 1944.

The volume of deliveries continued to grow and it became necessary to increase the manpower and 'horsepower' of the section. New companies arrived at the station bringing with them personnel and vehicles, They were quickly utilised and became part of the Station Motor Pool. By the end of 1943 the motor pool consisted of 89 vehicles and its own maintenance unit. At this time the vehicles were travelling an average of 60,000 miles a month. Deliveries of signal supplies were made daily to all parts of the United Kingdom.

By the end of February 1944 the section was able to move out of its shared quarters with the General Repair Section and into a building for its exclusive use. This arrangement included a private office for the Transportation Officer and an adjoining office for the dispatchers and drivers.

By March 1944 the Transportation Section was operating a total of 106 vehicles including Major Heartz's Canadian Utility Car, a machine shop truck, jeeps and a large number of G.M.C. 2 1/2 ton trucks. In April 25 bicycles were acquired, eight of which were put on hire for the use of the men to give them:

"plenty of good healthy recreation during off duty hours aswell as an opportunity to leisurely survey the surrounding countryside." *

The remaining 17 were used for official business, therefore reducing the number of jeep trips.

The section were proud of the fact that the vehicles from the depot had been involved in very few accidents during the first part of 1944. Two accidents were recorded in March and two in April. This was thought to be acceptable, considering that the vehicles were travelling an average of 80,000 miles a month in an unfamiliar country, without the use of roadsigns and often in blackout conditions. However in May, there was some dissatisfaction within the section over the number and state of the vehicles allocated to the station. Two small arms repair trucks, five 3/4 ton Dodge weapon Carriers and five jeeps that were considered to be surplus to the station were released. These vehicles, and in particular the jeeps, were not, in the section's opinion, surplus to requirement but nevertheless they were allocated to other bases. The jeeps were to be put to use within the 9th Air Force.

As a result of the high mileage clocked up by the remaining vehicles several had worn out parts and some of the replacements needed were unobtainable, In the previous winter several Ford 1 1/2 ton trucks had been obtained as the unit had not been able to acquire the 2 1/2 ton G.M.C trucks that it really needed. The Ford trucks had gradually lost nearly all usefulness, this was partly due to the poor

* History of Station 522.

John Blazek visiting Dudley Castle. (K. Bailey)

413, Hagley Road 1995. (M. Collins)

317, Hagley Road 1944. (J. Blazek)

condition that they were already in when they arrived at the depot. It was virtually impossible to obtain replacement parts for these vehicles. Requests were put in for additional 2 1/2 ton trucks but these were refused on the grounds of unavailability.

Ordnance Subsection.

During May 1944 there was an exchange of firearms at the base because of an order from Higher Headquarters. At the beginning of the month the majority of the 1903 Springfield cal.30 rifles of the 908th were exchanged for carbines cal.30. At the end of May all cal.45 Thompson submachine guns in the station were exchanged for 1903 cal. 30 rifles. Three cal.50 Browning machine guns arrived at the depot this month, these were the first to be received at the post.

During May a number of these firearms were required by the men at the base when taking part in the 'Salute the Soldier Parade'. This took place on Saturday 13th May 1944 in Smethwick, as it did in countless other towns across the breadth of the U.K. The men of the 908th and 892nd Signal Companies, carrying carbines, joined uniformed British troops in the parade. The U.S. troops carried the orange coloured airforce flag and the Stars and Stripes. The archivist for the 892nd records that this was:

"the first formal and public appearance of the 892nd Signal Company in the European Theatre of Operations.*

The British troops involved in the parade included R.A.F., Royal Navy, A.T.S. and the Police Force. The youth of the district were represented through the Navy League, Sea Cadet Corps of the T.S. Waterloo with their newly formed drum and bugle band, three divisions of the Smethwick Army Cadet Force with their bands, 494 Squadron A.T.C., Girls Training Corps and Junior Girls Training Corps.

The procession left Smethwick at 1530 hours and proceeded via West Park Road and St. Paul's Road. At Crocketts Lane civil defence and ambulance services joined with the parade. The units involved were: National Fire Service, Works fire brigades, St. John Ambulance Brigade and Cadets, Red Gross Society, Boy Scouts, Girl Guides and the Church Lads Brigade. The parade continued down the High Street to the Council House where the salute was taken by Rt.Hon. the Earl of Dudley, Regional Commissioner for the Midlands, he was assisted by Major Heartz from Station 522. The procession then proceeded via Bearwood Road to Lightwoods Park where it was dismissed.

Smethwick was aiming to raise a million pounds through the week's activities. This was to be used to equip and clothe eight British Infantry Battalions. By the Friday, when the Smethwick Telephone was put to press this figure had almost been realised.

*History of 892nd Company.

On June 22nd the 908th Company took part in a 'Salute the Soldier Parade' in the centre of Birmingham. The Salute the Soldier Drive in Birmingham was a huge success, raising seventeen million pounds to:

"-further assist the British Forces in the common efforts to crush the enemy." *

Communications Section.

On the opening of the base a request was submitted to the General Post Office to install a one person switchboard of the 5 plus 20 size. In addition two exchange lines with 12 extensions and two private speech lines were installed. A few months later, in February 1944 it was necessary to replace this switchboard with the larger 10 plus 50 size and two exchange lines were added thus decreasing the average time delay on calls.

In September 1943 a field switchboard (T.C.4) was installed with approximately 20 extensions because intercommunication between extensions were seriously interfering with service through the G.P.O. switchboard. By the end of December extensions were in use with plans being made to replace the present board with a T.C.2 Common Battery Switchboard. Two new field switchboards were installed in the early part of 1944, one of them in Defense Headquarters, thereby increasing the plant protection facilities. Service on the G.P.O. switchboard was maintained on a 24 hour basis while service on the field switchboard was only maintained during work hours. (0800 -1700 hours).

On November 5th, 1943 the teletype machine at Smethwick went into operation on a 24 hour basis and a new line was connected to the machine by members of the teletype repair and maintenance subsection. The majority of the advanced signal supply depots affiliated with Station 522 were already connected to this line, thus enabling messages to be relayed and received with minimum delay. The call letters S.K.A. were issued for the use of the depot.

In the early part of February 1944 the Depot Property Section aided this section in setting up the Message Center. The teleprinter and other equipment were moved so that all of the Communication facilities became concentrated in one location. This speeded up services and the delivery of messages. A new coderoom was constructed adjacent to the Message Center for the purpose of coding and decoding messages handled at the station.

The public address system was installed at the base in the first few months of 1944. This had two way speakers located at various sections throughout the depot and it was used for announcements ranging from gas, air raid and fire warnings to calls to 'Army Talks'. The General Repair Section were able to work alongside the Communication Section in setting up a system of superimposing speakers to a main circuit and thereby arranging for intercommunication between the various

* History of 908th Company.

Nissen Huts seen from Beakes Road. (Smethwick Local Studies Archives)

Nissen Huts in Beakes Road 1948. (Smethwick Local Studies Archives)

Headline of Smethwick Telephone 13/5/44.

departments of the Stock and Records Subsection of the depot.

In April the telephone line crew and line construction truck were used in setting up the two way radio antennae constructed with thirty foot poles to be used in establishing an American Forces Network Rebroadcasting Station at A.A.F. Station 158. Also in this month the crew were able to help Anglo American relations in the locality when they made available to the British Home Guard the construction truck to place and set 43 flagpoles. The flagpoles were for decoration purposes at a local fair held for the British Prisoners of War Fund.

Again in April the Communication section was designated to handle the repair and maintenance of teleprinter equipment for the 30 stations in the B.A.D.A. A teletype machine and repair shop were set up at the station to deal with the extra work. The shop was equipped for repairing and breaking down salvaged equipment and was outfitted with a spare parts section. The personnel for this shop consisted of six men who were being trained in repair, maintenance and installation work of this type.

In May 1944 Lt. Coleman succeeded Lt. Pratel as Communications Officer as the latter left for indefinite T.D. with H.Q. and H.Q. Sq. B.A.D.A., A.S.C., U.S.S.T.A.F.

General Repair Section

As the war progressed signal equipment became in short supply and therefore in May 1944 this section was given the added responsibility of salvage and reclamation whereas previously it was merely necessary for the section to list, test, repair or scrap equipment.

Plant Protection Section

In April 1944 Lt.Church returned from Anti-Gas School to launch an intensive training programme on the defence against chemical warfare. Lt.Church also carried out a close inspection on each man's gas mask equipment.

Medical Section

In May 1944 a Station Sick Quarters was opened in what was originally the Guard Room of the Depot. The number of medical staff was expanded to number two officers and five enlisted men. A dentist was also put on temporary duty at the post in May to inspect the men and give necessary dental treatment.

From this overall picture of Depot activities - - -

*"it can be seen that maximum efficiency in the performance of its mission by the Main Air Force Signal Supply Depot is a product of a smooth running machine whose integral parts are in themselves models of organisation. Add to this the valuable ingredient of high personal and group morale and you have a powerful contribution to the defeat of our enemies,"**

*History of Station 522.

Corporal Bob Howell, Medical Corps.

Chapter Four

Athletics. Entertainment, and Culture.

The Special Service and Education Sections played different roles to the other sections in the life at Station 522. The unit historian wrote in 1944:

"In the fields of athletics, entertainment and culture this office brought to the members of this station features of interest that it is felt serve also as considerable value in maintaining and strengthening soldier morale and health."

Education Section

In April 1944 the educational, historical and orientation duties of the station were assigned to C.W.O. Sorrentino who had recently been released from duty at Station 527 where he had been in Command of Detachment A of the 892nd Company. He replaced Lieutenant Lucas who left to assume duties as Warehouse Officer at Station 158. C.W.O. Sorrentino continued with the prepared programme of Army Talks which included such titles as: 'The British, are they human?' and 'How we are governed.' He also kept the station abreast of the latest war developments by the daily posting of war news on two large scale maps in the mess hall.

Correspondence courses were encouraged by C.W.O. Sorrentino. He also helped to organise educational classes on the base, such as the physics class conducted by Lt.Pfeiffer. In addition it was possible for the men to attend the Birmingham University 'Overseas Club'. In November 1944 26 enlisted men from the depot attended dancing classes there. Debates between military personnel and civilians were also held at the University, In February 1945 the subject for debate was 'Evil in the Cinema' and two enlisted men from Station 522 debated with two Birmingham University graduates on the subject.

Members of the units at Station 522 were asked to give talks on various subjects in the locality of Smethwick. In November 1943 Sgt.W.K.Davies was the speaker at a talk on the subject of 'America' at St.Chads Hall in Shireland Road. Forty G.I.s from the depot attended the lecture which was the last of a series of talks on 'The Allies' promoted by the Young Pioneers League. In his talk Sgt. Davies was keen to convince his audience that America was not a 'gum chewing nation'*

Lt.Wohlgemuth was asked to speak at the weekly meeting of the Smethwick Rotary Club several times. In February 1944 he spoke on 'Life and Conditions in the U.S.A.' and apparently the Rotary Club had 'seldom heard a more racy address'.# In his speech Lt. Wohlgemuth set out to explain that the average American differed

---

* Smethwick Telephone 27/11/43
# Smethwick Telephone 4/3/44

AMERICANS AND CHEWING GUM

The Americans are not a gum-chewing nation.

This fact—a direct denial of the common belief—was stressed at St. Chad's Hall on Saturday when the subject of the last of the present series of talks on our Allies promoted by the Young Pioneers' League was "America."

The meeting was attended by over forty Americans who are serving with the U.S. Forces in this country and proved the most successful of a particularly successful series that has included talks on Russia, Poland, Austria, Czechoslovakia, and modern Palestine. The statement concerning chewing gum was made in answer to many questions from the children. The Americans stressed that in their home country many of them never purchased chewing gum but while they are in England all troops are issued, free of charge, with a substantial ration of the sweetmeat which was apparently considered by the authorities to be helpful to the men. These statements should provide the complete answer to those who imagine America to be a nation of people with perpetually moving jaws.

Saturday's speaker was Sgt. W. K. Davis, who is training as a security officer in the U.S. Army. His home is at Providence, Rhode Island, America.

Mr. C. L. Conyers (treasurer of the League), who presided, was supported by the founder-chairman (Mrs. E. Seager).

In the course of his address, Sgt. Davis told how the dismissal bell for the end of school was no longer the signal for a chaotic rush to play, for many American children were so interested in their work that they stayed on until asked to leave by the teacher. There was a new way of teaching in which reading, writing and arithmetic were made meaningful and interesting and in which the child rather than the subject came first. New York's school system, he said, was experiencing an educational revolution.

The "activity programme" replaced to a large extent traditional classroom procedure. Children learnt by experience, deciding for themselves what they would study during the day, under the leadership of a class-chairman. Children were permitted to progress at their own speed and corrected their own papers, and if extra tuition were needed the teacher would spend time in a "skills" and drills class, but only for those pupils who did not know their work, and those who knew their work coached those who were not so advanced.

The new approach to teaching imbued the children with greater self-discipline, self-confidence, poise and willingness to assume responsibilities, and cultivated the creative talents of children. The children, teachers, parents and administrators were working to make democracy a living, vibrant force in the lives of young and old alike.

Smethwick Telephone 20/5/44.

Smethwick Telephone 15/1/44.

Smethwick Telephone 27/11/43.

Smethwick Telephone 4/11/44.

very little from the average Britisher except for the fact that sport in America was given a higher interest value than politics. Wohlgemuth did point out that the American housewife had more 'mod cons' (refrigerator, central heating' telephone) than the British housewife, although the writer of the article in the Telephone was doubtful of the advantage of having a telephone in the house. Lt.Wohlgemuth also expanded on the benefits of living in the wooden frame houses which are so popular in America, being simple and inexpensive to build. The Smethwick reporter thought that this was a good idea, one in which Britain could follow America's example after the war. The writer obviously did not have good foresight as frame houses have never really suited Britain's climate, although nowadays the majority of British houses do have a telephone!

Rotarian, John Fallon, concluded the talk by stating:

*"The speaker has at least shown us that America and England have a common sense of humour. We are inseparably bound together as nations and it will be to our mutual advantage to continue the wartime union in days of peace." **

Also on the subject of academia, the unit was able to join in the celebrations for the Shakespeare Festival month in April 1944 by taking weekly visits each Wednesday, to Stratford to attend the plays throughout the season. Transportation was provided for around 25 men each week. As the historian for the 908th company commented:

"A genuine interest in Shakespearean productions by a large percentage of the personnel reflects the high intellectual and cultural standards of the organisation."#

Special Service Section

In June 1944 Lt.Wohlgemuth took over from W.O.J.G. 'good do' Washburn as Special Service Officer. Washburn had been given his nickname by Lt.Pfeiffer at a dance that Pfeiffer sarcastically termed 'a good do', Instead of the bevy of beautiful girls Pfeiffer was expecting he found the affair to be strictly of the 'stag and bag variety.'* This American figure of speech can be translated by your imagination.

One of the first duties Lt.Wohlgemuth was given in his new capacity as Special Service Officer was to establish educational and recreational features at the new headquarters of the 908th Company. (202,Hagley Road). Books, magazines and athletic equipment were installed there. In August the Special Service moved into a new building. This had space for office staff and a dayroom containing tennis table and library.

Wohlgemuth also installed facilities for a photo film service so that the men could have their photographs processed on the base instead of sending them to

* Smethwick Telephone 4/3/44
# History of Station 522

Thimblemill Baths 1995. (M. Collins)

London. A small number of enlisted men operated the service voluntarily while the Base Intelligence Officer carried out the censorship. In the first ten days 50 rolls of film were received by the photo film service, During July 1944 257 rolls of film were processed and in the next month the figure increased to 486 rolls.

During May 1944 the Special Service brought out a newsheet entitled the 'Five Two Two Bullettin'. The editors hoped that this publication would:

*"go a long way towards strengthening unity, not only among our men but also between our men and officers."**

The first issue contained a message from Major Heartz in which he reminded the men of their vital contribution to the imminent invasion:

*"We're as vital as the veins in a body through which blood must flow. Yes, we are the Forces life blood itself. The equipment we pack and hurry along to its destination spells the difference between victory and defeat, between life and death for our men who fight in the air and on the ground."**

In September of this year the men were given the opportunity to use their journalistic abilities when the Special Service put up a 'Bulletin Board' where the

*History of Station 522.

American Red Cross Club in New Street, Birmingham 1944. (C. G. Hinde)

men could air their views in any field they wished. In the next month two enlisted men's newspapers, one entitled 'The Wallpaper', made their appearance on the board.

The Special Service Section was responsible for organising several sporting events. Drill periods and off duty hours would find the men engaging in American and English style football, volleyball, softball, baseball and 'horseshoes'. In April 1944 the Special Service was given the use of a ball field at Lightwoods Park Extension. Intersectional basketball, softball and baseball leagues were formed, In June the shift of personnel at the base resulted in a revision of the athletic schedule and a new softball league was organised based on the geographical States from which the men originated.

Games were played on Mondays and Thursdays when the men would be transported to the park in trucks. Once there, leaflets explaining the rules of the American games were distributed to the British spectators. Angela Macquire, a teenager at the time, remembers that the games used to draw large crowds. She recalls that it was:

"another first for us, but a very exciting game."

Another local resident remembers hearing a bugle being blown to signal the truck's departure at the end of the game. He also recalls that not all of the G.I.s came to the park with the intention of playing softball or baseball. He recalls that some men left their baseball kit lying on the ground and amused themselves by chasing the girls who had turned up as spectators for the match.

During 1944 various sporting fixtures were arranged. The men from the base were invited to play football and cricket against local teams. They also played basketball against teams from other American bases in the area. On the August bank holiday the Americans challenged the Canadian Army to a baseball match to be held at 'The Hawthorns' (West Bromwich Albion's football ground). Proceeds from the entrance money were to go to the benefit of the Red Cross Prisoners of War Fund and the Mayor of West Bromwich's Comfort Fund.

In September the men were privileged to see the well known Light Heavyweight, Billy Conn, in the Smethwick Drill Hall. The show was attended by several of the local dignitaries and Home Guardsmen aswell as the Station G.I.s and their guests.

Throughout the period that Station 522 was manned by Americans the Special Service was kept busy organising entertainments or the men and ensuring that they were able to attend functions in the locality of the base and in Birmingham. In January 1944 the men were able to attend a Red Cross Concert which featured a 'Lead the Band' contest. This was won by a corporal from Station 522. Also in January, and again in April, the Special Service Section from the U.S. 10th Replacement Depot from Whittington Barracks, Lichfield, produced a show on behalf of the Young Pioneers League. The Y.P.L. was a charitable organisation that

The Windsor, now a snooker club 1995. (M. Collins)

*The Rink, now a
Bingo Hall 1995. (M. Collins)*

provided children with activities and also took them on holidays. These shows were held at Thimblemill Baths Assembly Hall and, according to newspaper reports,* were of a high quality.

The Special Service Section from the 10th Replacement Depot was to return several times to Smethwick in 1944 to stage shows. In March the section produced a show at Thimblemill Baths in aid of the Local Fund for the Soldiers, Sailors and Airmen's Families Association. In June it performed a concert at the Empire Theatre. This was in aid of the Mayor's £3,000 appeal for the Duke of Gloucester's Red Cross and St.John fund. The show was well appreciated by the inhabitants of Smethwick although it must be pointed out that not everyone appreciated the 'swing music' of the band. But:

"for those with an ear for something a little more tuneful the pianoforte solos of James De Martini and the singing of a delightful bass - - - will remain outstanding memories."#

On November 14th the 10th Replacement Depot put on another show for the Y.P.L., this time it was entitled 'Let's Be Buddies' and it was held again at Thimblemill Baths. The proceeds from this show were £90, and this helped to provide parties for 400 Smethwick children, 200 wounded soldiers and the old age pensioners in the almshouses (£90 went a long way in those days!). In 1945 the unit returned to Smethwick to hold an Anglo American Friendship Ball and Cabaret. This time the proceeds from the event were donated equally between St.Dunstans (a charity for blind servicemen) and the Y.P.L.

Back in February the Smethwick Baths in Thimblemill Road had been the scene of a dance and cabaret act produced by the Special Service Section of Station 522. This dance was organised by a number of enlisted men from the unit who had instituted a 'social fund' for such occasions. The committee of Sgt.R.Guetschow, Sgt.J.Carplan and Sgt.W.Lindberg invited officers, girlfriends and the English families who had opened their homes to the men of the unit. The Mayor, Mayoress and Deputy Town Clerk were among the local dignitaries who joined the 500 guests at the dance.

On 15th June a dance was held at Birmingham Town Hall for all signal depot personnel at A.A.F.522, A.A.F.527, and A.A.F.158 and their guests which included W.A.C.s from the 1st Base Post Office in Sutton Coldfield and A.T.S. girls. The dance was hailed as a colossal success. As the historian recorded:

* Smethwick Telephone.
# Smethwick Telephone 24/6/44

WINDSOR

Mon., Tues., Thurs., Sat. from 2.0.
Wed., Fri. from 6.0.

— FOR SIX DAYS —

CARMEN MIRANDA, MICHAEL O'SHEA in
SOMETHING FOR THE BOYS (U)
with **VIVIAN BLAINE** (The Cherry Blonde)
(In Technicolour)

LINDON TRAVERS & JOHN WARWICK in DOUBLE ALIBI (A)

To-night : ARSENIC AND OLD LACE (A)   SUNDAY at 7.0 : LADIES IN RETIREMENT (A)

PRINCES

Mon., Tues., Thurs. from 2.30. Wed.,
Fri. from 6.0. Sat. from 5.0.

Monday—

GEORGE FORMBY
in —
Get Cracking (U)

Full Supporting Programme

Thursday—

TYRONE ANN
POWER BAXTER in
Crash Dive (U)

ANIMAL WONDERLAND (U)

To-night: MARKED MAN (A).   SUNDAY at 7.0: A NIGHT TO REMEMBER (A)

EMPIRE

Mon., Tues., Sat. from 5.0. Wed.,
Thurs., Fri. from 6.0.
To-night : JANIE (U).

Monday—

WALLACE JAMES
BEERY GLEASON in
This Man's Navy (U)

Full Supporting Programme

Thursday-

BILLY CAROL
HARTNELL RAYE in
Strawberry Roan (U)

Pat Parrish, Jackie Moran in
LET'S GO STEADY (U)

MAJESTIC

Mon., Tues., Sat. from 5.0. Wed.
from 2.30. Thurs., Fri. from 6.0.
To-night : JANIE (U).

Monday—

GRETA GYNT, GEOFFREY HIBBERT
JOYCE HOWARD in
The Common Touch (U)

Thursday—

ANN SHERIDAN, DENNIS MORGAN
JACK CARSON, IRENE MANNING in
Shine On,
Harvest Moon

Smethwick Telephone

48

Prince's, now a vacant building 1995. (M. Collins)

"A sincere feeling of gratitude has been expressed by the men for the extremely generous way the Lord Mayor of Birmingham and his various departments have assisted in the successful planning of this event, especially for the loan of Birmingham's beautiful, spacious Town Hall and facilities, further cementing the already unbreakable bonds of Anglo-American relations. "*

The Special Service Section formed its own dance band in April 1944 from seven members of the 892nd Company. W.O.J.G.washburn obtained the required musical instruments while Pfc.Frank Farelli directed the band. The musicians played at the various civilian functions that U.S. soldiers were invited to. They performed at the American Red Cross Club in New Street, Birmingham, on Decoration Day for the benefit of British wives of American soldiers. They also played at a 908th Signal Company dance in June where the:

"band and icecream were the most important attractions."#

The men from Station 522 also attended dances at the Coliseum in Bearwood Road. This former cinema housed a furniture store at the front of the premises and a dance hall at the rear. After the war the premises were used as a ballroom. It has since been demolished and a petrol station now occupies the site.

The area in the neighbourhood of the base was fortunate enough to boast nine cinemas and although the depot had its own movie projector the G.I.s often frequented the local picture houses to see the latest Hollywood films. The nearest of these to the base was the Windsor in Bearwood Road. This cinema had been opened in 1930 as a cinema although it also had a stage. After the war it became a variety theatre and well known personalities such as Des O'Connor trod its boards. Later it became a skating rink, and after that a snooker club.

The other cinemas in the area to be used by the G.I.s were: The Cape Hill Electric Theatre; The Majestic in Rutland Road; The Gaumont in Windmill Lane; (Incidentally the first cinema in the town to show 'Talkies'.) The Grove in Dudley Road; The Beacon in Brasshouse Lane; the Warley Odeon in Hagley Road West; Princes in High Street and the Smethwick Empire in St.Pauls Road. The latter of these was also designed to function both as a theatre and a cinema. Three of the above buildings have since been demolished and, although the others all serve useful purposes within the community for functions ranging from shops to a Sikh Gurdwara, not one is used as a picture house and there is no longer a cinema in Smethwick.

* History of the 908th Company.
# History of Station 522.

The Grove, now a builders merchants 1995. (M. Collins)

The Beacon, now a vacant building 1995. (M. Collins)

Smethwick Empire, now a Sikh Gurdwara 1995. (M. Collins)

The Abbey, 1995. (M. Collins)

The Thimblemill, 1995. (M. Collins)

The Kings Head, 1995. (M. Collins)

The Americans also used to spend their off duty time in the pubs in the locality. Favourite hostelries were: The Abbey in Abbey Road, The Thimblemill in Thimblemill Road, The Kings Head in Lordswood Road and The Red Cow, The Barleycorn and The Bear all in Bearwood Road. (The latter of these had a rather dubious reputation.) The Red Cow had been built in 1937 to replace one of the same name that had stood since the early eighteenth century. The G.I.s soon acquired a taste for the English beer which at first they found weak, watery and warm.

One of the local firms still in existence today, Masons, also tried to accommodate the American tastes in a less intoxicating beverage. Titus Mason had originally established his career in bottling ale, but at the beginning of the century he began the manufacture of mineral waters. In 1921 the company took over a large premises in Grantham Road and by 1938 the firm had developed into the largest producers of mineral waters in the Midlands. They were equipped with a modern automatic plant and employed over 100 staff.

The sugar rationing during the war caused production to be affected and a section of the factory was used to manufacture munitions. Production increased again when the U.S. Government awarded Masons the contract to manufacture and bottle Pepsi Cola for the American forces in Britain. Scarce ingredients such as sugar were supplied by the Americans on a daily basis, although the paper shortage meant that the bottles went unlabelled. The finished product was collected by the U.S. Army who distributed it to the various U.S. bases around the country. Masons also commenced the production of a pink American Cream Soda which was very popular with the American Servicemen.

As a contrast to the Pubs the churches in Smethwick also became a meeting place for the local people and the G.I.s. As has been noted Station 522 did not have its own chaplain but was visited on alternate weeks by Catholic and Protestant chaplains from other bases. Because of this the G.I.s were often to be seen at the churches in the locality of the depot where they became friendly with members of the various congregations, and in fact, they were welcome reinforcements to congregations reduced in number by the war.

Several G.I.s attended Bearwood Baptist Church in Bearwood Road. As well as Sunday Services the church held a number of social evenings which the Americans were invited to, On Mothering Sunday (May 7th) in 1944 the men assembled at the Baptist Church for services. Col. Arthur S. Dodgeon, Senior Chaplain of the U.S.S.T.A.F. conducted the services on that occasion. Later an informal party was held for the officers and their guests at the depot. The station band furnished the entertainment for the evening.

A number of G.I.s worshipped at St. Gregory's Catholic Church in Three Shires Oak Road. The men were transported in trucks to Mass. Angela Maquire recalls that:

"It was good to see them there, they even served on the altar occasionally."

The Barley Corn, 1995. (M. Collins)

The Bear, 1995. (M. Collins)

The Red Cow, 1997. (M. Collins)

St. Gregory's Church, 1995. (M. Collins)

Coliseum, 1929. (S. Smith, Smethwick Local Studies Archives)

Bearwood Baptist Church, 1964.
(Joseph Russell, Smethwick Local Studies Archives)

The church held a youth club after the evening Benediction service in the Guild Room adjacent to the church. Nora Crosbee (nee Hancox) remembers:

"A few Catholic Americans came to our church, then hearing music they came to see what went on . They liked what they saw and were welcomed by us members, boys and girls. They enjoyed it and brought their friends, plus the latest records from America, The fact that some of them were not Catholics did not matter, we, as youngsters of the Host Country, did our best to make them feel at home."

Angela remembers that she had her first nylons, biro pens and Dentine chewing gum from the Americans that attended the Youth Club. She also recalls that the Americans would buy enormous amounts of fish and chips from the local shop and bring them along to the Youth Club to share.

The Special Service Section and Education Sections were intent on helping the men to fit into the community in Smethwick, an environment very different from their home surroundings. The functions of this section were perhaps not essential to the war effort, but nevertheless important to young men thousands of miles from home who needed recreational facilities to keep up their morale.

Chapter Five

Anglo-American Relationships

The Special Service Section were keen to promote good Anglo-American relationships in and around Smethwick, and, for their part, the people of the district were, on the whole, ready to make the G.I.s feel welcome, particularly in the first few months of the existence of the depot. In October 1943 Major Heartz had the opportunity to thank the people of Smethwick when he was invited to be a guest of the Rotary Club at the Red Cow Hotel.

The Smethwick Telephone reported that:

> *"Major Leslie C.Heartz - - - is in command of a detachment of the United States Air Force stationed 'Somewhere in the Midlands".**

The Telephone goes on to report Major Heartz's words:

> *"My men have been simply deluged with kindly invitations during their stay here. The hospitality of British folks is really overwhelming - - -. We have enjoyed the greatest cooperation from both the military authorities and the civilian population wherever we have been stationed - - - and the offers of hospitality have been a great help because the facilities we have at our present headquarters permit of little in the way of entertainment outside duty hours. The many friendships we have made really mean a lot to us who are thousands of miles from our native land and we hope that they will be continued long after the war is forgotten."**

From the outset the people of Smethwick showed their hospitality to the men of Station 522. In September 1943, when the men had been at the base only a month the unit was the recipient of a gift of fruit and vegetables collected by the school children of Bearwood Road Council School. The American soldiers demonstrated their appreciation by sending generous contributions from their sweet rations to be distributed among the children and also promised to give them a Christmas party.

As promised the Christmas party took place at the school, much to the excitement of the children. An article about the party was featured in the Smethwick telephone under the heading:

> *"Gee, it was Some Party."**

* Smethwick Telephone.

Smethwick Telephone 15/1/44

Clarence Lenville jnr. on a visit to friends in Portland Road, Edgbaston. (N. Crosbee)

60

The Telephone reported that:

*"Christmas has been made a most outstanding occasion through the generosity of a unit of American soldiers."**

For several days preceding the party the G.I.s had been sending to the school toys of all kinds (184 in number) and 912 jars of sweets of every variety. The group of American officers and enlisted men who were guests of honour at the party brought with then 15 gallons of chocolate ice cream in large jars and 400 doughnuts supplied by the Mess Section at the base, They also brought a V.I.P. As the Telephone reported:

*"Perhaps the most welcome visitor of all for the children however was Pfc. E. Neumeister who appeared as an impressive but most genial Father Christmas. His was the most pleasant task of the day - that of distributing a toy to every one of the children in the lower classes and packets of sweets to the elder boys and girls - a fitting culmination to a delightful afternoon."**

The headmaster of the school, Mr. J.B. Goodwin, sent a letter to the newspaper expressing his appreciation for everything the Americans had done for the children. He finished by remarking:

*"Such service and generosity should be more widely known and will certainly do much to cement and secure the bonds of friendship between our two countries."**

Perhaps because the Americans had worked so hard to make sure that Christmas was a happy one for the young children at Bearwood School, many of the local inhabitants invited the soldiers to spend Christmas in their homes. After the festivities W.O.J.G. Washburn wrote to the Smethwick Telephone to thank the residents of Smethwick for their kindness.

A year later, in 1944, Christmas parties were also given at some of the local schools. Over two thousand children enjoyed Christmas music by the Station band and received gifts of candy and gum which the men contributed from their weekly post exchange rations. The following month the men of the 892nd Company had another encounter with the children of the district. The historian for the 892nd lightheartedly recounts the incident:

"Due to inclement weather we were unable to have very many road marches, however on one road march the company was 'attacked' by the local children with snowballs. We had to stage a strategic withdrawal; casualties were very light."#

* Smethwick Telephone 25/12/43
# History of the 892nd Company

The G.Is became substitute 'uncles' for the children of the district. Many of them were probably missing nieces and nephews, some even sons and daughters of their own. Several locals who were children at the time remember pressing their faces against the wire netting that surrounded the camp and calling out: "Any gum chum?" The men would usually oblige the youngsters and then ask them if they had any older sisters. Pamela Cashmore (nee Antcliff) remembers the soldiers riding around Bearwood in jeeps, throwing out packets of chewing gum and sweets to the local children.

Ivy Royall remembers that she had to go up to the Thimblemill Garage to ask the M.P. on duty there to refrain from giving her two year old, Janet, chewing gum as she was unused to it and rather than chewing the gum she was swallowing it. From then on the men gave her chocolate and candies.

The G.I.s became very fond of the English children and towards the end of 1943 they decided to 'adopt' a war orphan, According to the official records this was:

*"the nearest and dearest project attempted that year."**

To enter the adoption scheme it was necessary for the men to subscribe £100 to 'Stars and Stripes' (American Forces Newspaper) War Orphan Fund. They were allocated seven year old Irene from Sheffield, Although she wasn't able to see very much of her new G.I. uncles she visited the base on Thanksgiving Day in November.

The following March the men decided to 'adopt' a second child, this time they opted for a boy. They sent a second £100 to the War Orphan Fund and adopted ten year old Johnnie from Walsall Wood whose father had been killed by an enemy bomb in September 1940.

On Easter Monday (April 10th) 1944 Johnnie was the guest of honour at the base. he was escorted to the depot by an officer of the American red Cross and welcomed by a sign on a large placard saying: "Welcome Johnnie, from your Yankee Doodle Daddies." The station band played throughout a meal of fried chicken and pineapple ice cream.

*"After what was probably the biggest meal he had seen in years he was presented with a complete new outfit of clothing and a number of games and, to his delight, a football (English style)."**

Later he had a ride in a jeep and watched a Western Movie and a game of baseball. As anticipated Johnnie thoroughly enjoyed the day with his American friends, as the historian remarked:

*"Johnnie returned to his home - - - a tired but happy youngster - - -To say he was merely pleased is an understatement,"**

* History of Station 522

Corporal John Blazek visiting the Thompsons
L-R Mrs Ada Thompson, Margaret Green, John Blazek, Audrey Payne,
Kathleen Thompson. (K. Bailey)

John Blazek visiting the Thompsons.
(K. Bailey)

Eddie Allen visiting the Thompsons.
L-R Muriel Payne, Kathleen
Thompson, Eddie Allen. (K. Bailey)

Allan Brown visiting the Thompsons. (K. Bailey)

The Smethwick Telephone saw the two adoptions as a way for the men to express their appreciation of the British hospitality they had received in Smethwick and Bearwood. The Telephone reported:

"The Americans who have received a warm welcome from the people of the town in which they are stationed are anxious to show their appreciation of many kindnesses. The adoption of these two British children is one of the ways they have chosen to express their gratitude. It is a noble way of saying 'Thank you' and one which will go far towards tightening the bonds of Anglo American friendship."#

The G.I.s also worked towards tightening the bonds of Anglo American friendships through their relationships with the teenagers of Smethwick and Bearwood. Nora Crosbee and Angela Maquire both became friendly with American soldiers through St. Gregory's Youth Club. A couple of G.I.s occasionally walked 15 year old Nora home from the youth club as she lived en route to the camp. Her father (who had relatives in America) suggested that she invite the men into their home. She remembers:

"This I did and eventually these young men came to look upon our house as their home. If they were at a loose end they would say to each other: 'Let's go home.', knowing that they would be warmly welcomed."

Sixteen year old Angela's parents often asked one or two G.I.s to their house for meals. One of them felt particularly at home there. Angela recalls:

"I remember one in particular who never seemed to want to go back to base. My mother would say tactfully: 'What time do you have to get back, Flick?' 'Oh, anytime before reveille' was his answer, which dismayed my mother who didn't want to leave me, her 16 year old daughter, alone with him after midnight! He usually ambled off around 12:30 a.m."

Margaret Parry also attended St. Gregory's Youth Club although she met G.I. Alfred Louie King (known as Louie) when her 16 year old brother, Bert, invited him home to tea. Bert had met Louie and a couple of other G.I.s in Lightwoods Park and had started chatting to them one Sunday afternoon.

Margaret remembers that her mother was horrified when Bert brought Louie (a Chinese American) and his friends round the back of the house and into the yard. Margaret's mother had never met an oriental person before and immediately started worrying about what she would give him to eat. She needn't have worried as his favourite food seemed to be celery. After this occasion Louie spent most weekends with the Parry household. As Margaret says:

Smethwick Telephone 15/4/44.

"He became a fixture."

She remembers that Louie took her and her mother to the Hippodrome to see Irving Berlin in 'This is the Army', and that they threw a 'coming of age party' for Louie when he became 21.

Another teenager, Brian Gastinger, met G.I. Grover Pearson from Arkinsaw on a number 6 bus. Brian recalls that the bus was full and the only available seat was next to a G.I. He sat down and a conversation was struck up. By the end of the journey Grover had been invited to tea with Brian's family. British larders didn't boast many provisions in wartime but the Gastingers were ready to share the little they had with this friendly American who was far away from his own family.

Subsequently Grover invited Brian to the base each week for Sunday lunch. Brian remembers that he was offered fried chicken and real coffee, Grover also invited his English friend to 202, Hagley Road where he was billeted. Brian remembers that this was the first time that he ate fruit cake and cheese together and he emphasises that the cake was made with real fruit. He also recalls that the Americans seemed to have 'everything' but were willing to share with their English friends.

Peggy Padwood, 15 at the time, remembers the G.I.s as being:

"- - -most courteous, charming (and) generous. They were very generous with their money, very kind, always giving out presents - especially nylon stockings, which were like gold in those days."

Mrs. Purslow also recalls the generosity of the Americans to her family. She became friendly with two G.I.s after her husband had met them in a local pub, They had the unlikely names of 'Big Joe' and 'Little Joe', one being tall, the other short. She recalls that:

"Big Joe used to bring us tins of fruit juice and butter and whatever he could help us with. At Christmas he sent to America for presents for my family."

He presented the family with toys for the four children and gifts for Mr. and Mrs. Purslow. Mrs. Purslow still has a fountain pen that she received and an embroidered knitting bag that Joe's sister had made for her.

Mrs. Purslow also recalls the pair's sense of humour, One snowy winter evening she heard the doorbell and opened the door to find Big Joe in Little Joe's overcoat and vice versa. She remembers:

"It was hilarious. They certainly brightened our dreary war days."

Unfortunately not all of the people of Smethwick were hospitable to the Americans, The Smethwick Telephone reports on 20 May 1944 that three men were fined £5 at the Law Courts for 'baiting G.I.s', or, as the law put it:

*"- - - unlawfully fighting and provoking another person to fight."**

Superintendant A.J.Challiner made it plain that the Americans had given the police no trouble at all but they were continually being accosted by hooligans of this type. The chairman, R.W.Wilson, told the defendants:

"This baiting of American soldiers has got to stop. They are here to help us and people like you don't seem to appreciate it."*

Brian Gastinger suggests that some Smethwick residents resented the G.I.s because they were part of a non-combatant unit (although some men from Station 522 were later called into combat duties), whereas many of the local men were away fighting. Apart from this it is only natural that there would be some jealousy of the G.I.s who seemed to have all the luxuries while the Britons were trying to cope on their limited rations. There is a story that when the G.I.s arrived in Smethwick, tired and travelworn it was suggested that they should change into clean uniforms and send their old ones to the Criterion Laundry for dry cleaning. The story goes that the G.I.s declined the offer and decided to merely discard their dirty uniforms. This story has probably been grossly exaggerated but it does illustrate the way that some Smethwick people viewed the Americans.

Fortunately the G.I. baiting was not a regular occurrence and, on the whole, the people of Smethwick and Bearwood enjoyed a good relationship with the Americans.

* Smethwick Telephone 20/5/44

Chapter Six

G.I.Brides.

The arrival of the G.I.s in Smethwick created quite a stir amongst the teenage girls of the district who had never encountered a 'real live American' before, The only Americans they had previously seen were on the big screen on their weekly visits to the local cinemas where Americans were depicted as heroes of the wild west or tough fast talking gangsters.

When the Americans arrived they swept the girls off their feet with their nasal accents and their outgoing personalities. Kathleen Bailey remembers that they were more 'forward' than the traditionally reserved British. She lived opposite Station 522 in Beakes Road and remembers the unit arriving at the depot. No sooner had the trucks carrying the G.I.s pulled up at the pinafore factory than a couple of soldiers opened the garden gate and walked up to the window where she and her friend were sitting. When one of the neighbours saw them chatting she felt that it was her duty to go and tell Kathleen's mother that her fourteen year old daughter was flirting with the Americans!

The flirting was not always welcomed. Twelve year old Jean Dean did not enjoy being wolf whistled, although she admits now that if she had been a few years older she probably would have appreciated the compliment more.

Many parents forbade their daughters to have anything to do with the Americans. Unfortunately, as is often the case, the actions of the few had given the G.I.s a bad reputation regarding their relationships with young girls. At least one illegitimate baby with an American father was born in Smethwick and this created a scandal at the time. Ivy Royall remembers that there was an unlit passageway which led between the houses from Rawlins Road to Reginald Road. This was nicknamed 'the Baby Walk' for obvious reasons.

Getting pregnant was not the only risk the girls faced when going out with Americans. The U.S.Forces encountered problems with V.D, nationwide and therefore the United States War Department adopted strict control measures to prevent the spread of this unpleasant disease. From August 1944 onwards there was a purge on V.D. at Station 522. Captain Ward was appointed to the post of 'Station Venereal Disease Control Officer' and he took various measures including meetings, movies and lectures on the subject of V.D. to check the ailment. He also asked the Depot Property Section to turn out numerous V.D. posters and charts. At the end of the year the historian was pleased to announce that:

"The venereal disease rate hit a low during the month of December with no cases reported at all. It is believed that the classes and continual reminding of the men of the dangers of V.D. has helped immeasurably to keep it under such control." *

* History of Station 522

In the early part of 1945 the Medical Section was kept busy showing V.D. training films and a physical examination was given to all enlisted personnel under 31 years of age. (Officers and men over 31 were obviously thought not to be prone to this complaint.) During January there was one case of V.D, in the 892nd Company and this resulted in the company being confined to base for the evening. Kathleen Bailey remembers John Blazek calling through the fence to ask her to give a message to his fiancée, Margaret Green, to tell her that he wouldn't be allowed off base that night because one of the boys had been 'careless'. The historian records the following on this incident:

" - after all the talking and training films and the 'Pro-run' at night, he had to be careless and contract Gonorrhoea, but the new treatment with penicillin does a marvellous job and he is pronounced cured, "*

In October 1943 a more serious sexual incident had occurred when a Private from the base was charged with raping a Bearwood teenager. An American General Court Martial (the first of its type in Smethwick) was held at the civilian law courts when Private Charles D. Johnson was charged with a:

" - serious offence against an eighteen year old girl and also with unlawfully carrying a concealed weapon - a sheath knife."#

This was recorded under the headline:

"SMETHWICK'S FIRST COURT MARTIAL.

Serious Charge against American Soldier

Bearwood Girl's Story of Alleged Knife Threat!"#

It was reported in the Smethwick Telephone that the girl had told the court that she left home around 8:30 p.m. with three other girls. They went to one of the G.I. billets where the girl talked to Johnson until about 10:00p.m. when the girls decided to go home, Johnson then asked the girl to come behind a building with him as he was responsible for ensuring that this building was locked. The couple made love there, then the girl went to carry on home but at this point Johnson threatened her with a knife and forced her into a field where he allegedly raped her. The girl then went home crying. Johnson testified in his defence that he had been with her but not threatened her. As to the presence of the knife he explained:

"We all carry them where we come from,"#

* History of Station 522.
# Smethwick Telephone 23/10/43.

and he stated that he hadn't used it to threaten the girl but it had fallen out of his pocket so he had placed it on the ground alongside them. He told her brother shortly after the event:

*"I was only gaming, I didn't mean to do any harm to your sister."**

In Johnson's defence was the fact that the girl had consented to sex with him previous to the offence. The outcome of the trial was not reported in the newspaper and one is left unsure as to whether Johnson was guilty of the offence or not.

This is the only incident of this kind recorded in the area although the Smethwick Telephone reports many unions of happier kinds. The first wedding between an English girl and an American from the base took place in February 1944 at St.Chads Church in Shireland Road. Staff Sergeant Fred V.Green from Billings, Montana, married Stella Hazeldine from Waterloo Road. The bride:

*" - wore a gown of white satin and white silk tulle with a head-dress of white gardenias and veil and carried a bouquet of daffodils and lilies of the valley."**

The bridesmaids' dresses were of pale pink cobweb lace with head-dresses of pink flowers and they carried muffs with violets.

The groom had Captain J.A.Mayo as best man with Captain John W.Walch and Master Sergeant V.A. Freeborn as groomsmen."*

The reception was held at the Red Cow Hotel and the couple had their honeymoon in Stratford on Avon.

Olive and Walter Lindberg were not fortunate enough to have a honeymoon. Their wedding was planned for June 3rd 1944 and around this time all leave was cancelled as the men were confined to barracks due to the imminence of D.Day. Fortunately Master Sergeant Lindberg and a few close friends were given a 24 hour pass to attend the wedding.

Olive Doggett first met Sergeant Lindberg at her grandmother's birthday party. For Olive it was love at first sight and after the party the couple started meeting on a regular basis. After a brief courtship the couple were married at St.Marys Church in Bearwood Road. Olive had saved up her clothing coupons to purchase a blue dress and jacket from Jones in the Great Western Arcade, Birmingham. To match it

*Smethwick Telephone 23/10/43.
* Smethwick Telephone.

L-R Arthur Doggett (brother), Olive and Walter Lindberg,
Margaret Doggett, Dick Guetschow.

Marriage of Walter
Lindberg and Olive
Doggett. (M. Doggett)

she bought a blue hat trimmed with burgundy from C & A. Margaret Doggett, her sister in law, was her Maid of Honour, and to compliment Olive she wore a burgundy outfit trimmed with blue.

The reception was held at the Cape of Good Hope at the bottom of Cape Hill. Fifty to sixty guests attended although wartime shortages meant that the wedding breakfast was not as lavish as she would have liked. To celebrate the Anglo-American theme the table was draped with both the Union Jack and the Stars and Stripes. It was almost impossible to get wedding cakes made during wartime mainly due to the sugar rationing, so Olive had a cardboard cake, as many wartime brides did, with a much smaller cake concealed inside it.

Margaret Green was fortunate as her sister, Molly, was married to a grocer. Molly was able to bake a wedding cake for Margaret's wedding to Sergeant John Blazek, while her husband provided some of the other delicacies for the reception.. The rest of the food had to be gathered together little by little for the big day by Margaret's mother and sisters, but as Margaret says:

"It turned out quite well with enough food for all."

Wedding of John and Margaret Blazek
L-R Rev. Trendbath, Colonel Heartz, Eddie Allen (best man),
Jo Green (Margaret's neice), John Blazek, Margaret Blazek,
Ralph Green (Margaret's eldest brother), Doreen Willets (Margaret's Neice),
Margaret's Father, Margaret's Mother.

Margaret had met John one Sunday evening at the end of June 1944, John and his two friends, Allan Linwood Brown (Brownie) and Eddie Allen had become friendly with Margaret's friend's parents, the Thompsons. Mr and Mrs Thompson would often invite the three Americans to their home to listen to records and to generally enjoy the atmosphere of home from hone. In turn the Americans would do what they could for their English friends. Eddie's mother used to send packages of dress material and nylons to help the Thompsons out, as like all English families, they were clothing the family using a limited number of clothing coupons.

On this particular Sunday evening the three G.I.s, Kathleen Thompson and Margaret Green met at Bearwood Baptist Church and went to Kathleen's home after the service. After the group had listened to some records and chatted Margaret made a move to leave. John insisted on walking her home although she was reluctant for him to do this. On reaching Margaret's house John asked her out for a date but, in an attempt to deter him, she told him that he would have to phone and ask her the next day. Not to be dissuaded he did this and the phone was answered by Margaret's mother who handed the receiver straight to Margaret even though she was indicating to her mother to say she wasn't in. John had managed to get the couple tickets for a show at the Hippodrome where Vera Lynn was singing. Contrary to her expectations Margaret thoroughly enjoyed the evening and she reflects:

"After that night I did not seem to date anyone else but John."

Following that first date the couple spent as much time as possible together going to dances or the cinema. They also enjoyed walking and cycling around local places of interest, sometimes cycling as far as Stratford Upon Avon.

In October of 1944 John took Margaret into Birmingham and bought her an engagement ring. On the bus on the way back home he put it on her finger. Both of Margaret's parents were pleased and gave the marriage their blessing but before Margaret could marry John the Padre, Reverend Trendbath and two of John's officers had to come to the house to give her a formal interview, When the three officers were satisfied, it was necessary to complete various forms before the marriage could take place.

The couple were married at 3 p.m. on November 11th 1944 by Reverend E.G. Chapman. Originally the date was to be in December but Major Heartz warned the couple that John may be moving out before that date so the wedding was brought forward a month. Margaret and her bridesmaids had to borrow dresses as she remembers there were:

" - no coupons for those kind of fancy clothes."

Margaret and John's was the first G.I. wedding to be held at Bearwood Baptist Church. Margaret's brother gave her away as her father was too ill at the time. Margaret remembers the day clearly:

Margaret and John Blazek. (K. Bailey)

L-R Audrey Payne, Eddie Allen,
Muriel Payne. (K. Bailey)

John Blazek. (K. Bailey)

"It was a typical November day, drizzle and cold, but (it was) a happy day."

Several of the officers including Major Heartz, attended the wedding aswell as John's friends and Margaret's family and friends. 120 were invited to the reception which was held in the church hall. As John did not move out until the following August he was allowed to live at Margaret's home after the wedding.

Muriel Payne also met her husband to be at Kathleen Thompson's house. Kathleen's mother, Ada, worked at Taylor's Chemists in Cotteridge where she was assisted by Muriel. When Ada told Muriel about the three G.I.s that came over to her house to listen to records Muriel was keen to come over and meet them. So, one evening, Muriel and her sister cycled over from Kings Heath to the Thompson's house in Beakes Road. Muriel and Eddie Allen soon struck up a friendship but unfortunately Eddie was already engaged to a girl from his home town in Indiana. He did not feel that it was fair to break off the engagement by letter so he and Muriel decided to wait until the end of the war to get engaged.

Ada remembers Muriel coming to her house to wave off Eddie when he was moved out in September 1945. When Eddie got home and broke off the engagement he sent for Muriel and twelve months later she travelled over to the

State of Indiana to get married.

A large number of Anglo-American weddings took place in the various churches around the Smethwick area, Most G.I. brides had a fairly uncertain start to their married life. Because of the high casualty toll in the Battle of the Bulge some men from the depot at Smethwick were sent for combat training so that they could replace the large number of casualties at the front. Even the men left at the base did not know how long they had left in Smethwick before they were moved out or moved back home to the States. After V.E.Day the authorities began the operation to send the soldiers back home or to the Pacific Theatre of Operations. Many had to leave their English brides behind them and did not see them again for a year or, in some cases, two.

Olive Lindberg had to wait until 1947 to be able to travel over to the States to Join her husband. She sailed over on the Queen Mary with her daughter, Virginia, who was two by this time.

Walter Lindberg lived in Houston, Texas, but Olive found the climate in Houston too hot so the couple moved to Seattle. Olive still found it hard to settle down so after two years they returned to England and lived in Park Road, Smethwick, for four years or so while Walter worked for Cincinnati in Erdington. This time it was Walter who found it hard to settle down so he signed himself on board a ship at Liverpool and worked for the family's passage back to the States.

Margaret Blazek remembers her journey to America as being both exciting and frightening. She caught a train in February 1946 to Tidworth Barracks in Wiltshire where the G.I. brides were processed before they could travel to the States. She stayed at the barracks for about four days then she was bussed to Southampton and shipped out also on the Queen Mary. Since the brides were designated cabins alphabetically she was lucky enough to be placed in a first class cabin, although she had to share it with six other girls and a baby.

She remembers that the crossing was not too bad although she was seasick for a couple of days. The boat arrived in New York on March 1st. All night long the names were called out of brides whose new families had travelled to New York to meet then. The next morning Margaret and the remaining brides were taken to Grand Central Station where she caught the train for Cleveland, Ohio.

Margaret was designated a sleeper and she dined in the train, Being unfamiliar with American money she was unsure of how much to tip the waiter but she comments that she thought that the waiter made out quite well as all the brides tipped him. At 6:00 a.m. on Sunday March 3rd the girls were wakened early and at 7:00 a.m. the train arrived at Cleveland. Margaret's husband, John, and her father in law were waiting for her. They drove to John's parent's home at Berea where the couple were to live for the next few months. Lil, John's stepmother, had a welcome breakfast waiting for Margaret. John took her on a sightseeing trip and on a visit to his brother and sister in law. In the evening the rest of the family came to meet Margaret.

Margaret remembers that her new family were very kind but it still took her over a year to get over her homesickness. She has recovered from this now and at the present time, lives in Ohio with John. They have three children, eight, grandchildren and three great grandchildren.

Chapter Seven

Behind the Man at the Front Lines
(June - December 1944)

"The month of June will long be remembered by the people of the world but its dates will be even more firmly engraved on Station 522, in the warehouse on Beakes Road, Smethwick, Staffs, England, away from the booming guns, pounding channel surf and dive bombing planes, the announcement on the sixth day of June was one of those rare moments when the soldier who deals in supplies suddenly feels the significance of his job graphically brought home to him. He feels that much closer behind the man at the front lines."*

This is how the historian at Station 522 felt that the depot was involved in D Day, albeit behind the scenes.

The date of D.Day was a closely guarded secret before the event, but although the precise date was unknown the men of the base knew at the outset that something was in the air. On the first day of the month signal supply officers of the first, second, third and fourth Strategic Air Depots held a conference at Station 522. The purpose of the meeting was to clarify certain signal supply issues in order for procedures to run smoothly after the invasion of France.

The first indication to the men that the Normandy landings were about to take place was on the night of the fifth of June when a large number of aircraft was seen over the Midlands area en route to the Continent., John Blazek remembers seeing the sky filled with planes.

The next morning an announcement came over the public address system at the depot and all personnel were summoned to the shipping floor where Major Heartz mounted a platform to speak to the men.

"He reminded them of the seriousness and magnitude of the task that lay ahead of them and how really small was the demand for sacrifice of time and pleasure from them when compared with the many supreme sacrifices being made at that moment across the channel."*

He also hinted that this historic event would affect the men at the station because it would be necessary to bring about some changes.

*History of Station 522.

On the bulletin board over the next few days there were notices announcing the transfer of men from the 892nd Company to the 908th Company and vice versa. Transfers occurred at frequent intervals usually in groups of 15 to 20 at a time. Almost all of the personnel were relieved from their present assignments. Apparently the favourite question among enlisted men and officers at this time was: "What company are you in?" The effect of the transfers was to leave the two main groups with very few of the original personnel but assignments to the companies kept them almost up to previous strength so that all functions of the depot were able to operate normally.

The general shift of both commisioned and enlisted personnel began on the 7th of June. Detachment A of the 908th based at Station 158 was deactivated, twenty of the enlisted men were returned to their parent organisation at Station 522 while fifty were transferred to the 892nd Company.

On the 9th June the 879th Signal Company Depot, Aviation, consisting of four officers and 83 enlisted men arrived at Station 522. This company had travelled to Smethwick from Dinton, Wiltshire via A.A.F. Station 802, with their Commanding Officer, Major Lilburn G. Payne. Not all of the men in the group were to be stationed at Smethwick. Detachment B, consisting in the beginning of 14 men (soon to rise to 60), was based at Station 158 while five men were to be sent on indefinite temporary duty to Sudbury, Suffolk.

The 879th Company also became involved in the transfers of men that were occurring at Station 522. By the end of July the duty roster stood as follows:

Major L.G.Payne	Commanding Officer
1st Lt.R.D.Baker	Company Commander
1st Lt.N.K.Clarke	Detachment A Commander.
1st Lt.G.Saunders	Base Signal Officer A.A.F.802.
1st Lt. F.P.O.Malley	Assistant Signal Supply Officer.
2nd Lt. H. B. Jurecka.	Detachment D Commander.
2nd Lt.H.E. Church	Plant Protection Officer (transferred from 892nd)
2nd Lt.L.J.Wohlgemuth	Special Service Officer. (transferred from 892nd)
2nd Lt.H.V.Pfeiffer	British Radar Supply Officer T.D.A.A.F. 802.
2nd Lt.P.R.Ulrich	Indefinite T.D. at A.A.F.174.

The enlisted men of the company were assigned to the various sections as they were needed.

Changes among the officers in the 892nd included:

Major Heartz	promoted to Lieutenant Colonel on 1st July.
1st Lt.G.H.Coleman	Company Commander, Station Adjutant and Personnel Officer.
2nd Lt.R V Shaddy	Acting Company Commander of the 892nd.
2nd Lt.L. D. Epstein	Assistant Depot Signal Supply Officer in charge of shipping.
W.O.J.G.Washburn	Station Motor Transportation Officer and Ordnance Officer.
W.O.J.G.Thiery	Stations Communications Officer.

Meanwhile the 908th Company were given orders to move to a new location at Welsh Farms, Harborne and to spend some time preparing to support the invading army by providing supplies at a nearer source (i.e. from a base in France). On the 19th June the entire 908th Company, consisting of eight officers and 205 enlisted men marched to their new living quarters:

"This move was primarily for the purpose of field training and physical conditioning of the company in preparation for future operations."*

For the next week the 908th spent the morning at the base in Smethwick then returned at noon to Harborne.#

In addition to the amending of the units and personnel stationed at A.A.F. 522 D.Day brought a change in priorities at the station. The depot now had to consider supplying airfields on the continent.

After D+20ß it became the policy of the depot to prepare a series of shipments of major airborne signal equipment to the 9th Air Force in France. This equipment went directly to the air force depots. The shipments were spaced at ten day intervals and were automatic, requiring no individual requisitioning by the actual units.

By August the establishment of the 4th, 5th and 6th Tactical Air Depots in France meant that Station 522 shipped directly to one control depot in France operated by the 900th Signal Company. In the same month the warehouse personnel began preparing shipments for the 5th Base Air Depot which was also being set up in France. By December this Base Air Depot had still not been established therefore Station 522 was instructed to ship all equipment to Continental Air Depot A.A.F. 389 (Compeigne).

* History of Station 522
# See Appendix 4 for future operations of the 908th.
ß 20 days after D Day.

Around this time all Eighth Air Force, Ninth Air Force and Base Air Depots were instructed to turn in to Station 522 all signal supplies not necessary to their requirements in the next month. This brought about two problems. The first was that Ninth Air Force Tactical Depots were being sent to the Continent at short notice, giving the units very little time to sort out their excess supplies. It became necessary to send detachments of men from Smethwick to the vacated air bases to finish off the Job.

The second problem was the lack of storage space at Smethwick. This dilemma was primarily solved by sending some unnecessary equipment straight back to the United States, some to Communication Zone General Depot G.18*, and some to the British Depots.

Another factor to increase the storage problem was the fact that Station 522 was designated the main storage site for teletype spare parts. All units were instructed to turn in all stocks other than their immediate requirements to Station 522.

In September a new station was established at Constitution Hill, Sudbury, Suffolk, designated as A.A.F. 382. Personnel from Smethwick had begun to operate at Sudbury, in July 1944 in a building formerly used as a corset factory. Because the work there was expected to last only 30 days a small group of men with one officer was sent there on temporary duty. Their task was to receive, store and distribute chaff.* When it became evident that higher headquarters was planning to use the Sudbury Depot as a point for long period storage, instead of a mere stop gap for a temporary surplus, Detachment A of the 908th Company, consisting of two officers and seventeen men plus two attached were assigned there.

* The Continent.
#Also known as window. Metallised strips dropped by aircraft and designed to Jam radar.

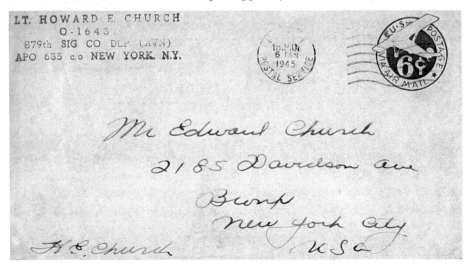

Letter sent home from Lt. Church after his transfer into the 879th Company.

In November a site outside the immediate vicinity of Smethwick was found that could give the extra storage space. This site had 26 hangars with 40,440 square feet of inside storage space and 186,000 square feet of outside storage space. This would give twice the area previously occupied.

As one might expect the Transportation Section also reported accelerated activity after D Day. The pace was kept up under adverse conditions as many of the vehicles were past their best and in need of parts it was almost impossible to obtain. The unit historian referred to the Transportation Section's problems:

"The invasion of the continent with its consequent requirements has made it even more difficult than before."#

To add to the difficulties there was an acute shortage of tyres at this time. In August ten K53 Dodge Radio Trucks were converted into cargo vehicles and in October the section attempted to coordinate trips and cut down traffic as much as possible thus reducing wear and tear on the vehicles.

The Transportation Section were proud of the small number of accidents involving vehicles from the base. The historian suggested that this was partly due to the many safety posters adorning the motor pool office. These encouraged the men to:

" - adopt caution as a watchword."#

In August vehicles from the depot were involved in six accidents but the base historian was quick to point out that the accidents:

" - were of a minor nature, and in every instance were the fault of the other parties involved rather than our own drivers."#

In October the section adopted a policy of not driving after dark, as previously most accidents had happened at night in blackout conditions.

In July the depot had acquired several new vehicles. Amongst them were six jeeps which were to be allocated one to each section as far as possible. The depot also acquired a Wolseley Staff Car for Lt.Col.Heartz. This was long overdue as he had been awaiting a vehicle since the opening of the depot. On its arrival the Transportation Section set to work to put a shiny black finish on it.

Towards the end of September the 2194th Quartermaster Truck Company arrived at Station 522 to run the Transportation Section. Those drivers formerly assigned to the Motor Pool were assigned new duties. The new company were to take over the hauling and delivery of all signal supply freight.

#History of Station 522.

It would appear that the 2194th was a negro company. Several residents of Smethwick remember trucks with black drivers being parked on either side of Beakes Road, Prior to the war the people of Smethwick had not encountered black people and some were rather suspicious of the men in this unit at first. One schoolgirl remembers coming face to face with a black G.I. and then running home to her mother, crying. Her mother forbade her to return to that spot. Needless to say the next day saw the girl returning with her friends so that they could get a closer look.

The 2194th occupied the barracks at Welsh Farms recently vacated by the 908th. As their historian, Hyman Malley, recorded:

"The place was in pretty bad shape but with quite a bit of work it has begun to look like a place for soldiers to live in. The boys are happy in their work of preparing a new home for themselves."

The Welsh Farms site boasted a Post Exchange, Dayroom, Mess Hall and space for a Motor Pool, The company expressed their hopes of getting a beer to sell in the dayroom. The Communication section furnished a B.D.71 telephone service with six extensions at the barracks.

By February of the following year the unit had improved their living quarters extensively. A new guard shack had been erected, hot water was piped into the shower room, and plans were even going ahead for an 18" high picket fence around the camp. The historian noted:

*"The morale is very high since the living and working conditions are so much better than ever before."**

Another morale booster that the historian noted was the fact that several good pubs were within easy walking distance for the men to get their usual mild and bitters.

On the arrival of the 2194th Company the historian for the 892nd Company noted:

"With the arrival of a new unit on the post, the dress and discipline is likely to go down to the level of the new unit but constant reminders this time has kept the 892nd discipline and dress up to its usual high standard."#

The fact that this type of comment was not made when other new companies joined the depot would seem to reinforce the idea that this was a black unit.

Speaking on behalf of the 2194th 1st Lt. Linindoll noted that although the unit was concerned with problems of administration, supply and having to learn the new station regulations:

*History of 2194th Quartermaster Trucking Company.
History of the 892nd Company

AAF 382, Constitution Hill, Sudbury, Suffolk.

"The problem wasn't as big as it had been at other stations at other times in that all concerned were very cooperative. All officers and enlisted men of the depot did everything possible to see that we had everything we needed." *

He also noted that:

"The morale of the organization is rather high since the working hours at this station are much less than at our previous station." *

Although the 2194th felt that they were working less hours at Station 522 the months immediately following D Day were particularly busy for the depot. From June until the end of the year the soldiers on the continent were battling hard and experiencing a high rate of casualties even after Paris was liberated in August, but the base historian was keen not to belittle the work of the men at Station 522 who worked hard to keep the air bases stocked up with equipment. The historian concludes the report of June 1944 with:

"Admittedly to the men of Station 522 the month of June may not have been as exciting as to the men who stormed the coast of Normandy, but it was a month that will live long in their memory." +

After D Day some security restrictions were lifted although it took until September for the order prohibiting the granting of furloughs to be rescinded. When furloughs were granted the historian for the 892nd noted:

"Many of the officers and men of the station took advantage of the opportunity to do some travelling and sightseeing in various parts of the United Kingdom." #

The historian for the 879th recorded that:

"The chief attraction of the recent lifting of furlough restrictions is the opportunity for a few days of well observed relaxation and should result in a more efficient prosecution of this particular company's portion of the war effort." †

On the 21st October Heartz was sent to Marseilles on a reconnaissance mission. he returned on the 27th and was able to tell the men about the conditions in France. In December Air Force Signal Storage Base Depot No.1 A.A.F. 158 (Sudbury, Derbyshire) was placed under Heartz's command along with Station 522.

* History of 219 4th Quartermaster Trucking Company.
+ History of Station 522
#History of 892nd Company
† History of 879th Company

Christmas rounded off the eventful year of 1944. Everyone at Station 522, except for a skeleton crew, had the day off. Although this was a festive time Captain Bader of the 879th noted:

*"Morale has tended to decrease slightly due to the advent of the holiday season. The season when all men feel the need for and long for home ties, efforts are being made to relieve the tension and homesickness that come at this particular time of the year."**

By this time one lucky man, Technical Sergeant Santhay of the 892nd had already been transferred to 596 Depot Group, Kelly Field, Texas. This had occurred on the 28th November, he was one of the first men to be transferred back to the States from Station 522.

Due to an alert from Christmas Eve the guard at the Station was doubled and two guards were placed at each of the houses that served as the men's quarters. On the 30th December the men were awakened by air raid sirens and later found that this was due to flying bombs in the vicinity.

The alert did not prevent the men from celebrating Christmas, The 2194th held their Christmas party on the 16th December. Hyman Malley describes the festivities:

"Much to the surprise of some people the party went swell with no trouble until the party broke up at 2330 hours. One of the boys had a little personal trouble and went a little off beam, He was placed in the Guard House after disobeying an order from the 1st Sgt. The main disaster of the evening was the beer shortage."#

This company seemed very concerned with the lack of beer generally. One hopes that 'one of the boys' slept off his 'little personal trouble' the next morning!

Captain Bader of the 879th finishes his report for December 1944 on a more positive note:

"Christmas, the second one in the European Theatre of Operations for most of us has come and gone, leaving behind memories of a two day holiday and a remarkable Christmas Dinner which was augmented by those rare delicacies received in packages from the United States. Festivities in many English hones were shared in by members of this organization - a homey touch which helped to alleviate the nostalgia we all felt. Parties and dances were the order of the day - the one order always obeyed willingly by both officers and men. But now comes the period of readjustment which always follows a short vacation - made a little easier this year because everyone feels that Christmas 1945 will be a happier one throughout the world and is, therefore, something to look forward to.'*

* History of 879th Company
# History of the 2194th Quartermaster Trucking Company.

Chapter Eight

Doubled Efforts. January - April 1945

The beginning of 1945 saw the Russian drive on Germany from the East and the Allied elimination of the so called 'bulge' on the Western Front. In February the Allied Armies started to clear the enemy from the West side of the Rhine and the air onslaught on the Reich assumed gigantic proportions. This was reflected in the activities at the Main Air Force Signal Supply Depot.

Because of the shortage of troops in the combat zone three men from the 892nd Company were transferred in accordance with the Infantry Reinforcement Programme in January. Several enlisted men of the 879th Company were also transferred during this month, Only one (Tec.4.Donald Paltridge) was a volunteer. Regarding the transfer of men the historian noted:

"All of the men realise that the transfer of rear echelon troops to infantry outfits and the probability that such transfers will become a routine matter will mean longer working hours and the necessity for doubled efforts on those men remaining in the United Kingdom. However one objects to, or shrinks from these changes, each man is determined to do his job, whatever it may be, to the best of his ability." *

More men were transferred to the Infantry Reinforcement Programme during the months following January, their losses were deeply felt, both from personal and operational standpoints. In April the base welcomed:

" - several combat weary and injured soldiers from the foxholes of Belgium and Germany to the placid existence of Birmingham and Smethwick - these men are grateful for the change as is evidenced by their willingness to cooperate and to fill in the gaps left by the departed men." *

H.Q. Section

On February 26th 1945 Lt.Col.Heartz and two other officers were relieved of assignment with the 892nd Signal Company and assigned to Detachment F, Headquarters and Headquarters Squadron, Base Air Depot Area. In March Heartz was assigned as Acting Signal Officer, Base Air Depot Area at A.A.F.590 (Burtonwood) during the temporary absence of Lt.Col.William H. Harrington.

* History of Station 522.

Storage and Issue Section.

The first few months of 1945 saw much reorganisation at Station 522 as surplus was sent to bases on the Continent, or to Liverpool ready for transfer back to the United States. During April all stock for A.A.F.527 was transferred to A.A.F. 158.

Transportation Section

The personnel were now responsible for transporting equipment from the various bases in the U.K to the Continent. Because of the shortage of trucking facilities it was necessary to transport some of the heavier equipment by rail to A.A.F. 802 where it could be transported by sea to Europe. Lighter equipment was picked up by trucks and taken to Grove, Berks. where it could be transported by air to the Continent.

During January the section decided to recover all the bicycles that had been issued to various individuals on the base as;

*"The weather is not conducive to cycling."**

The bicycles were put into storage, ready to be issued in the summer although their condition had already deteriorated due to rust and corrosion caused by the rain and snow.

In April the 2194th Truck Company was transferred to another station and the motor pool was returned to the same basis of operation that it had before. The personnel formerly working in the motor pool but assigned to different duties on the arrival of the 2194th were returned to their former assignments. Because of the departure of the trucking company with their own transport it was necessary to acquire more vehicles and so five 1 1/2 ton trucks were requisitioned by the base.

Ordnance Subsection.

This subsection worked in close cooperation with the Transportation Section and was responsible for ordering all automotive parts and the repair of some vehicles. Close coordination with the Ordnance Depot at A.A.F.590 meant that the section were able to obtain the majority of the necessary parts and by February 1945 there were no critical shortages.

This section were also engaged in manufacturing some of the intricate spare parts for the teletype machines as these were not readily available at this stage in the war.

The armourers of this section who were responsible for cleaning and repairing the weapons were commended by a visiting colonel who inspected the armourer's shop and found it to be the best he had ever visited.

*History of Station 522.

Communication Section

Because of the recent personnel changes this section was short of manpower therefore it was necessary to train more men. The men of the section were given the responsibility of instructing the novices in wire repair, teletype repair and maintenance, and teletype and telephone operating. Teletype machines and switchboards were set up for the men to practise on so that novices could sit in with the regular operators on duty to gain practical experience and confidence in operating.

In March one of the buildings at Welsh Farms was taken over by the personnel of the teletype repair shop and converted into a school. Training and instruction were given by the regular repair and maintenance personnel under the supervision of 'Tec.5.William F. Harper and Tec.5.Harry Migdal.

The class was divided into two, one group attended a lecture and discussion period while the other participated in a period of practical demonstration. The majority of the enlisted men giving instruction had not had experience of instructing before but as a large part of the course was practical work it was thought that both instructors and trainees would benefit from the programme. The students were given a weekly written test to check their progress, the average rating of the pupils came out as 'very good', which was seen as a tribute to the abilities and thoroughness of the instructors. In April the school was moved to A.A.F. 158 because of insufficient space at Station 522.

In April the B.D.71 field switchboard and its site extensions were removed from the Welsh Farms site. In doing so the team were able to recover the 1 1/4 miles of V.110-13 field wire used. All the materials were repaired, checked and returned to stock for future use..

General Repair Section

Because of the shortage of parts at this time this section found that it was necessary to manufacture special screws and miscellaneous parts for typewriters and radio equipment aswell as carrying out the general repair work.

Medical Section

From January to March 1945 Captain Ward found it necessary to prescribe sulfadiazene tablets for the men before the noon meal in order to counteract the development of colds.

At the beginning of the year heavy casualties on the Continent meant that large amounts of blood were required therefore a blood donor programme was initiated at Station 522.

On the 12th of April 1945 the men of Station 522 were shocked to hear of the death of President Franklin D.Roosevelt who died of a cerebral haemorrhage at

Warm Springs in Georgia. Lt.Col.Heartz

> " - summoned the men together to pass a few moments in prayer as a memorial tribute to the passing of a loved and respected leader of a great nation. From the neighbouring communities of Bearwood and Smethwick came many sincere messages of the heartfelt grief of the British people at the loss of a true friend."*

The men of the 908th Signal Depot Company, now based in Fontenay, France, also mourned the passing of President Roosevelt as 1st Lt.Clyde Underwood noted:

> "To the average member of the 908th, whether or not he was a political supporter of the President in life, the death of Franklin D.Roosevelt brought about a sense of personal shock.#

As in Smethwick, the men met together to hear Captain R. F. Keyworth read out the teletype message from the Secretary of War, which was followed by a five minute period of silent prayer. On a positive note Lt. Underwood remarked:

> "Despite this world and national grief, war operations went ahead to hasten the end of this European conflict."#

A thought no doubt echoed by the men remaining at Station 522.

* History of Station 522.
# History of 908th Company.

SMETHWICK TELEPHONE

SATURDAY, APRIL 14th, 1945

Printing and Publishing Offices:
24, HUME STREET, SMETHWICK, 40.
Tel. No.: SME. 0095

DIM-OUT—From 9.34 p.m. to 6.42 a.m.

DEATH OF PRESIDENT ROOSEVELT

President Roosevelt died suddenly on Thursday afternoon at the White House, the cause of his death, which occurred at Warm Springs, Georgia, was cerebral hemorrhage.

---

the aired ter." en of id it d. It pirit, hing. the were but good

CES
ig of
ibus
pany
some
been
new
, as
lder

...Mr. T. D. Waring, presenting the accounts, said the association would have finished the year with a small debit balance but for a

PRESIDENT ROOSEVELT

The Editor has received the following message from Lieut-Col. Leslie C. Heartz, Officer Commanding the U.S. Army Air Force Station.

Sir,—I wish to thank the citizens of Smethwick in behalf of the members of this Station for their kind expressions of sympathy on the death of our President, Frank Delano Roosevelt.—Very truly yours,

LESLIE C. HEARTZ.

legacy of £100 from the late Mrs. Dawes, so that the actual position was that there was a credit balance of £57 11s. 5d.

Alderman C. W. Taylor moved the re-election of the officers—Mr. I. Howard

For
Etheric
the inf
could b
notifica
Commis
added
yards
bombs
by lacl
only wi
be bon

"PU

The
Wedne
Woodc
curiou
manag
charge
and o
"I pr
officia
was of

Chapter Nine

Smethwick Celebrates Victory.

*"Five years, eight months and eight days of warfare on and over the Continent of Europe and on and under the waters around it had come to an end on May 8th 1945."**

"May, the month of victory in Europe, saw the realisation of an objective on which the eyes of the whole freedom-loving world would have been focussed for these long and burdensome years. The news of victory was received by the personnel of A.A.F.522 and its subordinate units with appropriate sobriety. Lt.Col.Leslie C.Heartz, the Station Commander, spoke to the assembled men and reminded them that their duties would continue and that they would probably remain in their present location for some time yet. Out of consideration to the British people to whom victory meant so much he ordered the men of his command to refrain from visiting the public houses on V.E.Day and the day following. The purpose of the order was understood and complied with by all the men."#

V.E. Day had been anticipated by the officers at the station and plans for recreational and educational events for the day and the 13 days following it were made prior to the event. Members of the Special Service staff attended the 'Soldier Show Demonstration School' at Base Air Depot Area to learn various show techniques to use in the 'post hostilities programme.'

On the evening of V.E.Day a dance with music played by the station band was organised, and this was held at the Smethwick Drill Hall. Teenager, Kathleen Thompson was one of the civilians attending the dance. Kathleen's father had asked G.I.Allan Brown to obtain two tickets for Kathleen and her friend, Christine Thompson.'Brownie' got the tickets and also arranged the transport.The girls were taken to the dance in an American Army truck and Kathleen remembers the difficulty she had climbing into the back of it.

At the dance everybody was celebrating and having a good time but Kathleen remembers being upset when one of the G.I.s showed her photos that he had brought back from Belsen Concentration Camp. She was shocked at the pictures of the mounds of corpses and the emaciated looking people who had managed to survive. Brownie was annoyed that the man had brought out the distressing photos at a celebration of victory but the photographer replied that he had taken the

* History of 908th Company.
# History of Station 522.

Residents at Pheasant Road and Norman Road, V.E. Party
Children on front row L-R
Geoffry Porter, Pamela Antcliff, Anthony Cross, John Antcliff.

View from other end of street. (P. Cashmore)

photos to show his family back home the truth. Kathleen remembers that it brought home to her the horrors of war, she reflects:

"I had come out of the war unscathed but so many people would not enjoy V.E.Day. Many had to die in order to end the Hitler regime."

The Smethwick Telephone reported on Smethwick's response to the announcement of Victory in Europe.:

*"In the few hours that elapsed between the radio announcement that 'Tomorrow is V.E.Day' and the actual day, Smethwick underwent a transformation, the like of which was only equalled at the Coronation eight years ago."**

Flags, buntings and streamers were arrayed from house to house across the street. Margaret Blazek remembers seeing red, white and blue streamers in house windows and flags everywhere. Most of the children wore red white and blue while the adults wore favours of these colours.

Unfortunately V.E.Day started off wet but apparently this did not dampen spirits. Many people ventured out to attend thanksgiving services at the local churches and to buy flags and bunting. Fortunately the weather brightened in the afternoon, the children were able to come out to collect wood for the bonfires and preparations went ahead for street parties. In the afternoon everyone stopped first to listen to the Prime Minister and later to the King on the radio.

In the evening the Council House was lit by an arrangement of floodlights, Fireworks lit the night sky and hundreds of bonfires were to be seen, When one bonfire ran short of fuel a piano that had been playing in celebration during the day was consigned to the flames. Effigies of Hitler were burnt on the bonfires or hung from lamp posts around Smethwick.

Over the next two days the festivities and street parties continued. Most roads had a party for the children. As the Smethwick Telephone pointed out the older folk realised that the war in the Far East was still to be won but:

*"The youngsters have endured much as a result of the war in Europe and have gone without many things which in normal times help to make childhood happy. That is all over now so that for them at least there was a cause for celebration."**

Street parties took place in many of the roads around Smethwick. Among the list were Pope Street, Montague Road, Merivale Road and Western Road. Pamela Cashmore (nee Antcliff), a seven year old at the tine remembers the street party that she attended. This involved the residents of Pheasant Road and a few from Norman Road. She and her sister remember eating spam sandwiches, home made

* Smethwick Telephone 12/5/45.

cakes, jellies, blancmanges and bottled fruit, She recalls being made to eat bread and butter with the bottled and tinned fruit:

"How I hated that combination,"

she comments. The food was followed by dancing in the street and also a large bonfire was lit in the middle of the road. Photographs were taken of the event and Pamela remembers telling her friend, Antony Cross, to pull a funny face as one of the photos was taken.

Ivy Royall remembers that her five year old, Janet, unfortunately had measles on V.E.Day. There was a street party in Katherine Road where they lived but poor Janet had to sit in her front garden to celebrate the event instead of being seated at the table in the road with the other children.

The Smethwick Telephone records that one aftermath of the two days of celebration was that by V.E.Day plus two most of the alcohol in the pubs of the district had been consumed and only mineral waters were available. The Rechabites, who held their annual meeting on the Saturday preceding the 8th May, made their views known on the issue of allowing the pubs to remain open an extra hour on V.E.Day. This, they pointed out, would prevent the staffs of the pubs from participating in home and public celebrations and would increase the work of the police. The group also disapproved of the fact that all ranks of H.M.Forces would be allowed to drink to celebrate victory. Judging from the celebrations in Smethwick very few people took any notice of the report from this meeting.

Meanwhile, in France, the 908th Company were also celebrating Victory in Europe. The men based in Fontenay took part in a Victory Parade along with other units in the area. They were flanked by thousands of cheering French civilians waving flags representing all of the Allied Nations.

Lt.Underwood recorded that the men of the 908th received the news of a European victory with 'marked enthusiasm':

*"It is right that the peoples of the civilised world should rejoice in this historic hour, as did the 'Yanks' along with the neighbouring French civilians for a big Job well done."**

G.I. John Blazek, with the 892nd in Smethwick, remembers the relief felt by everyone on V.E.Day. He recalls that he was:

" - overjoyed to see it all end but still mindful that there was another war still to finish."

Lt.Underwood, with the 908th, reflected that:

"As the men cheered the victory it was remembered that it imposed on us a sobering obligation - our continued efforts to crush the remaining Axis Partner in the Pacific. To

* History of the 908th Company

How Smethwick Celebrated Victory

Memorable Scenes in Decorated Streets

BONFIRES — STREET PARTIES — FIREWORKS

THE ADVENT OF VE-DAY FOUND SMETHWICK WELL PREPARED TO CELEBRATE IN A MANNER BEFITTING THE HISTORIC OCCASION. IT WAS PRIMARILY A DAY OF THANKSGIVING IN THE CHURCHES AND IN THE HOMES, AND OF CELEBRATION IN THE STREETS. THE CELEBRATIONS WERE NOT ENTIRELY UNBOUNDED, FOR THERE WAS A GENERAL RECOGNITION THAT THE FINAL CHAPTER OF THE WAR HAS YET TO BE WRITTEN. BUT REASONABLE REJOICING WAS A RIGHT OF THE PEOPLE WHO HAVE HELPED TO MAKE VICTORY IN EUROPE POSSIBLE.

The heavy rain of the early morning failed to dampen joyous spirits, and though there was little to indicate that this was the day for which people had waited for more than five and a half-years, except the bedraggled and trooping street decorations, folk went on quickly adding the last touches to the gaily-trimmed windows of their homes. Those who braved the weather and ventured into the streets did so in order to attend one of the many short services of thanksgiving that were held in Smethwick churches, or to complete a bit of last-minute shopping in preparation for two days' holiday.

As the morning wore on, the overcast sky lightened to give promise of a fine afternoon. With the passing of the storm-clouds came an air of happy anticipation. The promise was fulfilled, and the afternoon and evening provided a perfect example of an English May day. With the first burst of sunshine, streets that had been deserted became full of life and colour. Children wearing dresses and suits of red, white and blue, and adults sporting favours in the national colours thronged the footpaths and roadways, admiring the decorations and animatedly discussing their own plans for celebrating this day of days. In many roads, heaps of wood gathered from bombed sites, odd bits of broken furniture, dead branches of trees, were prepared in readiness for the evening's bonfire. Furniture and tables were dragged out for the children's parties; wireless sets and gramophones blared out of doors at full volume.

The afternoon brought a pause in the merrymaking. The Prime Minister's radio speech, in which he officially announced the end of the war in Europe, was heard with rapt attention and greeted with the cheers it merited. Then the celebrations went on with renewed zest. Singing, dancing, sports, bonfires, games—all were included, and with another pause for the reception of the King's

TO-MORROW'S CIVIC SERVICES

There is to be a civic service of thanksgiving to-morrow (Sunday) at Holy Trinity Church. The Mayor and Mayoress, together with members of the Town Council, corporate officials and representatives of local organisations are to assemble at the Council House at 10.15 a.m. and make procession to the church, where the vicar (Rev. A. Gordon Cooke) will conduct the service and preach the sermon. The procession will be re-formed after the service, and will disband at the Council House.

The Mayor and members of the Council are to attend Evensong at St. Mary's, Bearwood, privately. The Rev. J. G. Roberts, M.A., will be the preacher.

At Oldbury

To-morrow (Sunday) at 3.0 p.m., the Mayor of Oldbury (Councillor C. T. Barlow), accompanied by members of the Town Council, magistrates, public representatives and members of local organisations, will attend Oldbury Parish Church for a thanksgiving service.

P.O.W. RELATIVES' SERVICE

Members of the Smethwick branch of the Prisoners of War Relatives' Association are to attend the morning service at St. Alban's Church to-morrow (Sunday) to give thanks for the end of hostilities in Europe and the return of many former prisoners. The vicar (Rev. E. Edmonds-Smith, M.A.) will conduct the service.

COUNCILLORS CELEBRATE

At the invitation of the Mayor, members of the Town Council and chief officials attended at the Council House on Wednesday afternoon and enjoyed a social hour.

END OF THE WAR

How Japan's Surrender was Announced

Premier's Midnight Broadcast

The good news for which the peoples of the Allied Nations had been so anxiously waiting was given to the world at midnight on Tuesday. Japan had unconditionally surrendered. The announcement was broadcast simultaneously by Mr. Attlee, the Prime Minister, from Downing Street, by President Truman from the White House and by Moscow radio.

The Japanese reply to the Allied demands ran:—

"With reference to the announcement of August 10 regarding the acceptance of the provisions of the Potsdam Declaration and the reply of the United States, Great Britain, the Soviet Union and China sent by Secretary of State Byrnes on the date of August 11, the Japanese Government has the honour to communicate to the Governments of the Four Powers as follows:—

(1) His Majesty the Emperor has issued an Imperial rescript regarding Japan's acceptance of the provisions of the Potsdam Declaration. (2) His Majesty the Emperor is prepared to authorise and ensure the signature by his Government and the Imperial Headquarters of the necessary terms for carrying out the provisions of the Potsdam Declaration.

His Majesty is also prepared to issue this communication to all military, naval and air authorities to issue to all Forces under their control, wherever located, to cease active resistance and to surrender arms.

(Signed) Togo.

Premier's Statement

Mr. Attlee retailed the circumstances under which Japan, taking full advantage of surprise and treachery, fell upon the United States and Great Britain on December 7th, 1941. He proceeded:—

"Taking full advantage of surprise and treachery, the Japanese forces quickly overran the territories of ourselves and our Allies in the Far East, and at one time it appeared as though these invaders would reach the main and of Australia and advance into India. But the tide turned.

"With ever-increasing speed the mighty forces of the United States and the British Commonwealth and Empire and other Allies, were brought to bear. Their resistance has now everywhere been broken.

"At this time we should pay tribute to the men from this country, from the Dominions, from India and the Colonies, to our Fleets, Armies and Air Forces that have fought so well in the campaign against Japan.

"Our gratitude goes out to all our splendid Allies, above all to the United States, without whose prodigious efforts this war in the East would still have many years to run. We also think especially at this time of the prisoners in Japanese hands, of our friends in the Dominions, Australia and New Zealand, in India and Burma, and in those colonial territories upon whom the brunt of the Japanese attack fell. We rejoice that these territories will soon be purged of the Japanese invader."

Victory Holiday

The Prime Minister then announced the victory holiday on Wednesday and Thursday, adding: "When we return to work on Friday morning we must turn again to the great tasks before us. But for the moment let all who can relax and enjoy themselves in the knowledge of work well done.

"Peace has once again come to the world. Let us thank God for this great deliverance and His mercy. Long live the King!"

After Mr. Attlee's announcement the national anthems of Britain, the United States, the Soviet Union and China were played and then followed a short religious service.

Democracy's Great Day

After giving the news to a Press conference at the White House, President Truman addressed the clamorous crowd assembled outside and said: "This is a great day. This is the day we have been waiting for since Pearl Harbour. This is a day when Fascism finally dies, as we always know it would. This is a day for democracy, but our real task lies ahead. We are faced with the greatest task in our life—the task of ensuring peace, but I know we will do it too."

SMETHWICK GOES

Woods and Lightwoods housing areas were what one might describe as gay but not gaudy *see to it that never again will there be a repetition of the suffering, misery and chaos which was born of this war. To the peoples of Europe the grim task of reconstruction and their place again in a world family of nations."* *

Three months after V.E. Day the remaining Axis Partner was crushed and the war was finally ended. The Smethwick Telephone reported:

"The good news for which the people of the Allied Nations had been so anxiously waiting was given to the world at midnight on Tuesday (14th August). Japan had unconditionally surrendered. The announcement was broadcast simultaneously by Mr Atlee, the Prime Minister, from Downing Street; by President Trueman from the White House and by Moscow Radio," #

Mr. Atlee went on to describe the terms of the agreement and remind the people that:

"Our gratitude goes out to all our splendid Allies, above all to the United States without whose prodigious efforts this war in the East would still have many years to run." #

He then announced a victory holiday for the next two days. He concluded:

"Peace has once again come to the world. Let us thank God for this great deliverance and His mercy. Long live the King!" #

Simultaneously President Trueman addressed the crowd assembled outside the White House saying:

"This is a great day. This is the day we have been waiting for since Pearl Harbor. This is the day when Fascism finally dies, as we always knew it would. This is a day for democracy, but our real task lies ahead. We are faced with the greatest task in our life - the task of ensuring peace, but I know we will do it too." #

Kathleen Bailey remembers that V.J.Day was not celebrated in quite the same way that V.E.Day was. She recalls:

"This came earlier than we had expected owing to the dropping of two atom bombs on Hiroshima and Nagasaki. Two terrible events never to be forgotten. How dreadful war is. If only nations could live in friendship with each other."

* History of the 908th Company.
# Smethwick Telephone August 1945.

John Blazek remembers the elation he felt when he heard the news of V.J.Day. At the time he was at a staging area in France and was waiting to be transported to the Pacific Theatre of Operations. When V.J.Day arrived he was flown back to England where he stayed to assist in the closure of some of the American bases in Staffordshire.

John's wife, Margaret, remembers V.J.Day with mixed feelings. Naturally she was pleased that the war was over but seeing the troops returning home from the fighting reminded her that many of them wouldn't ever return, among them her older brother, Philip, who was only 21 when he was killed.

The people of Smethwick celebrated the end of the war in much the same way that they had celebrated Victory in Europe. As on V.E.Day the weather started dull but brightened in the afternoon. The bells of the Old Church rang out and the bunting and flags were to be seen in the streets. At the Council House each window was adorned with a shield flanked by flags, again the building was floodlit.

Processions of children paraded through the town, some singing, some playing dustbin lids. Lorryloads of singing children were also to be seen being driven around the area. Many of the roads organised street parties for the children. In Montague Road there was a maypole with dancers decked out in red, white and blue. A number of streets had dancing and people dressed in fancy dress. The Mayor and Mayoress made a tour of the decorated streets.

In the evening bonfires were to be seen this time with a Japanese effigy to take the place of Guy Fawkes. One wonders how the people managed to find anything to burn after the bonfires of V.E.Day had taken everything combustible. On the Sunday there were special services of thanksgiving for the end of a six year long conflict.

The archivist for Station 522 describes V.J.Day and its aftermath in the following way:

"Emblazoned in the annals of history the month of August 1945 ranks as the climax to the greatest era of destruction and devastation the world has ever known. But the untold suffering and privation of the free peoples of the earth have not been in vain, for now, at long last, the combined efforts and resources of the Allied Forces have brought about the final capitulation of our enemies. Exactly six years to the very day that we were plunged into the fiery cauldron of war, the Japanese envoys signed the surrender papers that brought peace to the war weary world and put an end to 'man's inhumanity to man'. Rising from the ashes and the rubble, the world once again focuses its attentions on the serious task of reconstruction." *

* History of Station 522.

Chapter Ten

Born of War, Died of Peace.

With the advent of peace in Europe operations at Station 522 were scaled down. The number of men at the depot was reduced and the remaining stock in the warehouse was dispatched as quickly and efficiently as possible. From May 1945 onwards transfer lists were posted on the bulletin board and a number of men were sent back to the United States.

The end of the war was also a time for looking back on the achievements of the men working towards the victory. In October 1944 Colonel Heartz had been awarded the Bronze star medal for:

*" - exceptionally meritorious conduct and the performance of outstanding services from September 1st 1942 to June 30th 1944."**

Apparently Heartz was not interested in taking the glory for himself:

"In a subsequent talk to the officers and men Lt.Col.Heartz reminded them that this award made to him as Station Commander was, in effect, a tribute to all of them for their participation in the project."#

A year later, in October 1945, Heartz was awarded the Croix de Guerre with Red Star for exceptional services in the operation for the liberation of France.

* Smethwick Telephone 18/11/44
\# History of Station 522.

Congratulations

LIEUT-COL. Leslie, C. Heartz, O.C. of the U.S.A.A.F. stationed in Smethwick, has been awarded the Croix de Guerre with Red Star for exceptional services in the operation for the liberation of France. Many will desire to congratulate this popular officer on his well-merited award.

Smethwick Telephone 20/10/45.

The 908th Company had also been given awards for their work over in France. The twenty men of Detachment C under the command first of Captain Keyworth, then Lt.Echelson were awarded the Bronze Service Star. This was for putting their lives at risk flying over occupied France to set up communications for the 12th Depot Supply Squadron. On 28th May 1945 Captain Keyworth and seven enlisted men received the Certificate of Merit for meritorious conduct and unselfish devotion to duty for the period of 1st January to 20th May 1945, Also Colonel Turner commended the 908th for the efficient and systematic manner in which the depot operated and recommended the company for a Meritorious Unit Plaque.

During June 1945 the 879th Company was gradually disbanded. On 18th June Detachment A (A.A.F.Station 802) and C (A.A.F. Station 169) were stood down. They were followed by Detachment B (A.A.F. Station 158) nine days later. A large percentage of the personnel of these detachments were transferred first to Station 522. On the 22nd June the Company received a movement order issued by Headquarters, European Theatre of Operations. The orders stipulated that the company were to make themselves ready to return to the United States on 10th July.

Around this time a group of 20 or 30 men arrived in Smethwick from Burtonwood to help close down the depot. This was the last unit to work at the depot and was known as Detachment F, H.q. and Hq.Sq.,B.A.D.A. Sergeant Doyle Dillon was in this group and has good memories of the mess hall where:

"My memory tells me that they served better food than we were accustomed to at Burtonwood."

He also remembers that:

"My relationship with the local people was excellent."

STORAGE AND ISSUE SECTION.

It was the duty of this section to distribute the stock still in the warehouse. All unfinished requisitions were cancelled while all supplies due to arrive were to be forwarded as requested unless otherwise directed. The forwarding of shipments arriving from the United States for the Eighth Air Force units was halted and any equipment that arrived was held within depot stock.

All meteorological supplies at the Station were packed and sent to the U.S. General Depot G.15, from there it was forwarded to the 925th Signal Company Depot, Aviation on the Continent who were now responsible for storage and issue of all meteorological equipment and supplies for the 18th and 21st Weather Squadrons of the Eighth Air Force and Squadrons of the Ninth Air Force.

All stock of British origin was returned to the British Authorities. From the remainder of the supplies some items were shipped to the Pacific for use in that

Theatre of Operations while the majority of signal equipment was sent to Base Air Signal Depot Oberwisenfeld, Germany. Any superfluous items were shipped back to the United States.

At one stage the repacking of equipment was halted due to the shortage of lumber in the U.K. It was necessary to submit requisitions for redeployment packing materials to enable repacking to continue. When the materials arrived the Depot Property Section was given the task of constructing packing cases.

COMMUNICATION SECTION

Aswell as the routine repair work carried out by this section the personnel were involved in disconnecting teletypewriters of the A.A.F. stations that were being vacated.

EDUCATION SECTION

Since January the Education Officer had been laying the groundwork for the Army Post War Education Program, interviewing the men to determine their requirements and desires, cataloguing them and selecting a tentative staff to instruct in the various subjects. In June the men were taken in groups of ten for vocational guidance interviews. These were carried out using an Army Vocational Information Kit.

After V.J.day the men of the 892nd Company began the process of being transferred back to the United States and the date for closure of the station was set for October 1st.

In September several of the men, including Master Sergeant Eddie Allen, were transferred to the 63rd Fighter Squadron, 56th Fighter Group at Boxted in Essex. At the end of the war this unit served as a 'holding group' for U.S.A.A.F. personnel awaiting the journey home.

Eddie remembers sailing on the Queen Mary on October 11th with the rest of the personnel from the 56th Fighter Group.

Doyle Dillon remembers that his unit finished closing down the depot around the middle of September when the men were shipped to A.A.F. 158.

Although the men were relieved to be going home to see family and friends that they had not seen or spoken to for two or three years it was with regret that they left behind the town that they had come to think of as their second home. On his departure from the base W.O.J.G.Washburn wrote to the Smethwick Telephone:

*"Sir - - - it is with a feeling of sadness that we leave this community where we have made many lasting friendships and where we have received such splendid cooperation from the civilian authorities."**

The people of Smethwick were also sorry to see the closure of the camp.

Margaret Parry remembers that her whole family wept when the depot ceased operations and the men moved on, as did Louie, the G.I. who had become a part of their family. Kathleen Bailey, who was 17 at the time, remembers standing outside her house in Beakes Road waving goodbye to two truckloads of men thinking that she would probably never see them again. She reflects:

> *"Beakes Road never seemed the same after they had departed. The day that they left the depot seemed more like a mortuary, it was too silent. No more cheerful waves as the boys passed by, no more marching in the road and no more dashing to get their chow."*

The historian for the base concludes the official archives for Station 522 in this way:

*Smethwick Telephone.
> *"And so we close what may very well be the last chapter in the history of A.A.F.522. A U.S. Army Air Force Station born of war, died of peace, but during its lifetime it has stood as a tribute to the men who helped to make it the fine and efficient organisation that has won praise from all who have come in contact with it."**

*History of Station 522.

Abbreviations and Terms

U.S. TERMS.

A.A.F   -   Army Air Force.

A.S.C.   -   Air Service Command, (Operating within the U.S.A. this organisation scheduled the air force equipment and supplies required by all overseas air forces.)

B.A.D.   -   Base Air Depot (see Appendix 2)

B.A.D.A.   -   Base Air Depot Area.

Comm. Z.   -   Communication Zone. (Area behind the combat zone.)

E.T.O.   -   European Theatre of Operations.

H.Q.   -   Headquarters.

M.P.   -   Military Police.

P.X.   -   Post Exchange. (Equivalent of British NAAFI,)

P.T.O.   -   Pacific Theatre of Operations.

Q.M.   -   Quartermaster.

S.A.D.   -   Strategic Air - Depot. (see Appendix 2.)

S.O.S.   -   Services of Supply.
Responsible for administrative, supply and service activities of the War Department in the U.K. Also responsible for extending the communication and transportation systems to meet wartime demands.

Sq.   -   Squadron.

T.A.D.   -   Tactical Air Depot. (see Appendix 2).

T.D.   -   Temporary Duty

U.S.S.T.A.F. - United States Strategic Tactical Air Force. (Officially established 1/1/44 under the command of Lt.Gen.Carl Spaatz). Held administrative responsibility for the U.S. Air Forces in the U.K.

W.A.C. - Women's Army Corps.

Assigned. - Having permanent duties at a station.

Attached. - Having temporary duties at a station.

Detached. - Detailed for special service.

BRITISH TERMS.

A.T.C. - Air Training Corps.

A.T.S. - Auxiliary Territorial Service. (British women's army).

R.A.F. - Royal Air Force.

Y.P.L. - Young Pioneers League.

APPENDIX 1.

U.S.A.A.F. STATIONS REFERRED TO BY NUMBER.

A.A.F.	158	Sudbury Derbyshire.
A.A.F.	169	Stansted, Essex,
A.A.F.	174	Sudbury, Suffolk.
A.A.F.	382	Constitution Hill, Sudbury. Suffolk.
A.A.F.	388	Marseilles, France.
A.A.F.	389	Compeigne, France.
A.A.F.	403	Kingston Bagpuize, Oxfordshire.
A.A.F.	404	Chilbolton, Hampshire.
A.A.F.	466	Membury, Wiltshire.
A.A.F.	470	Hitchen, Suffolk.
A.A.F.	479	North Witham, Lincolnshire.
A.A.F.	486	Greenham Common, Berkshire.
A.A.F.	505	Neaton, Norfolk.
A.A.F.	519	Grove, Oxfordshire.
A.A.F.	522	Smethwick, Staffordshire (now in Sandwell)
A.A.F.	527	Leicester, Leicestershire.
A.A.F.	547	Abbots Ripton, Cambridgeshire.
A.A.F.	582	Warton, Lancashire.
A.A.F.	586	Camp Griffiths, Middlesex.
A.A.F.	590	Burtonwood, Lancashire.
A.A.F.	595	Troston, Suffolk.
A.A.F.	597	Langford Lodge, N. Ireland.
A.A.F.	802	Baverstock, Wiltshire.

APPENDIX 2.

FUNCTION OF AIR DEPOTS: BASE, STRATEGIC, TACTICAL.

BASE AIR DEPOTS.

These were primary airforce depots situated away from combat areas for security reasons. Their function was to prepare new aircraft for combat units and carry out 4th echelon maintenance. This involved restoration of worn or damaged aircraft, periodic overhaul of assemblies and accessories, fabrication of parts, technical modifications and the organisation of reclaimed and salvaged materials.

B.A.D.1. A.A.F. 590. Burtonwood.
-specialised in maintenance work on B17 Flying Fortresses, P47 Thunderbolts and P38 Lightnings.
Work was also carried out on radial engines.

B.A.D.2. A.A.F. 582. Warton.
- specialised in maintenance on B24 Liberators and P51 Mustangs. Work was also carried out on inlines.

B.A.D.3. A.A.F.597. Langford Lodge.
-specialised in work on propeller overhaul and manufacturing modification kits.
Operations ceased August 1944.

B.A.D.4. A.A.F.802 Baverstock/ A,A,F.486 Greenham Common,
-operations commenced October 1944 to meet requirements of 9th Air Force.

STRATEGIC AIR DEPOTS

Strategic Air Depots served the 8th Air Force which was involved in strategic warfare, i.e. the destruction of sources of production and maintenance of the enemy's war efforts. The primary function of these air depots was to give 3rd echelon maintenance to the aircraft of the 8th Air Force. This involved carrying out repairs requiring mobile machinery and equipment. This included field repairs and salvage removal and replacement of major unit assemblies, fabrication of minor parts and minor repairs to aircraft structures. Modification of aircraft was only undertaken when the work could not be performed by the Base Air Depot.

S.A.D.l. A.A.F.595. Troston (Honington)
-responsible for B17 Flying Fortresses of the 3rd Air Division.

S.A.D.2. A.A.F.547. Abbots Bipton (Alconbury)
- responsible for B17 Flying Fortresses of the 1st Air Division.

S.A.D.3. AAF.505. Neaton (Watton)
- responsible for B24 Liberators of the 2nd Air Division.

S.A.D.4. A.A.F.470. Hitchen (Wattisham)
- responsible for fighter aircraft.

TACTICAL AIR DEPOTS.

Tactical Air Depots serviced the aircraft of the 9th Air Force which was involved in tactical warfare, i.e. targeting enemy forces and supplies. The prerequisite of tactical operations is to establish and maintain air superiority.

T.A.D.1. A.A.F.479. North Witham
- serviced C47 Dakotas, C53 (larger versions of Dakota)s and gliders.

T.A.D.2. A.A.F.169. Stansted
- serviced B26 Marauders.

T.A.D.3. A.A.F.519. Grove
- serviced Spitfires, A20 Havocs, P51 Mustangs, P61. Black Widows and F6 Lightnings (photo reconnaissance)

T.A.D.4. A.A.F.403. Kingston Bagpuize
- serviced P38 Lightnings and P51 Mustangs.

T.A.D.5. A.A.F.404. Chilbolton
- serviced P47 Thunderbolts.

T.A.D.6. A.A.F.466. Membury
- serviced P47 Thunderbolts.

OFFICER'S RANK BADGES

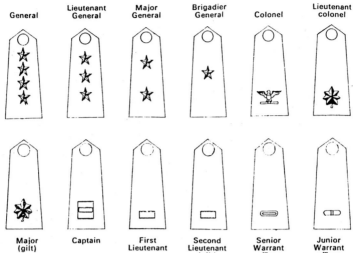

General	Lieutenant General	Major General	Brigadier General	Colonel	Lieutenant colonel

Major (gilt)	Captain	First Lieutenant	Second Lieutenant (gilt)	Senior Warrant officer	Junior Warrant officer

ENLISTED MEN'S RANK BADGES

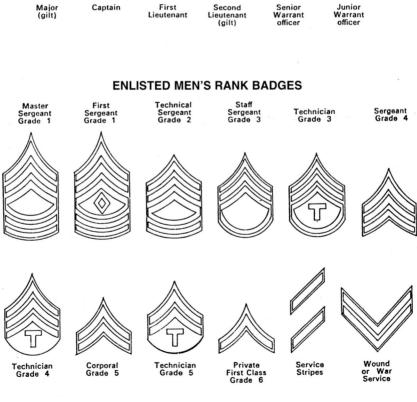

Master Sergeant Grade 1	First Sergeant Grade 1	Technical Sergeant Grade 2	Staff Sergeant Grade 3	Technician Grade 3	Sergeant Grade 4

Technician Grade 4	Corporal Grade 5	Technician Grade 5	Private First Class Grade 6	Service Stripes	Wound or War Service

APPENDIX 3.

Abbreviated Ranks.

Gen.	General
Col.	Colonel
Lt.Col.	Lieutenant Colonel
Maj.	Major.
Capt.	Captain
1st Lt.	First Lieutenant.
2nd Lt.	Second Lieutenant.
C.W.O.	Chief (Senior) Warrant Officer.
W.O.J.G.	Warrant Officer Junior Grade.
Sgt.	Sergeant.
Tech.Sgt.	Technical Sergeant.
Tech.4.	Technician Grade 4.
Cpl.	Corporal.
Pfc.	Private First Class.
Pvt.	Private.

APPENDIX 4.

MOVEMENTS OF 908th SIGNAL COMPANY DEPOT, AVIATION FOLLOWING ITS DEPARTURE FROM STATION 522.
June 1944 - June 1945.

1944
19th June. WELSH FARMS, HARBORNE.
(Mornings -duties at Station 522.)

25th June. CASTLE BROMWICH.
Training in use of weapons, map reading, military symbols, tent pitching, gas drill etc.
Attendance at schools in Principles of Electricity, Radio Operation, Radio and Radar Repair, Teletyping, Message Centre and Codework.

27th June.
Alerted for overseas duty, then stood down. Group given new Table of Organisation to work to.

September.
Group split into 5 detachments and moved out.

14th October.
Parent Organisation moved to MOSELEY, BIRMINGHAM.

DETACHMENT A. - 2 officers, 17 enlisted men under the command of 1st Lt. Leon D. Epstein assigned to A.A.F.382 to handle the storage and issue of window chaff.

DETACHMENT B. - 3 officers, 40 enlisted men under the command of 1st Lt.Clyde G.Underwood assigned to A.A.F. 158 to store and supply signal equipment.

DETACHMENT C. - under the command of Capt. R.F. Keyworth assigned to A.A.F. 388 to maintain signal communications in that area of France.

DETACHMENT D. - under the command of 1st Lt.Ganzert assigned to Compeigne, France, to operate the communication and supply system at that base.

DETACHMENT E. - 44 enlisted men under the command of 1st Lt.Stein assigned to A.A.F.169 (T.A.D.2) to maintain signal supply duties at that base.

DETACHMENT F. - under the command of C.W.O. Mancrief assigned to A.A.F. 519. (T.A.D.3)

13th December
- Detachment B disbanded and personnel transferred to
Detachment C, 879th Signal Company which remained at the same location. Detachments A and B join parent organisation at Moseley.

1945.

4th January
- First group of 908th Company depart from Moseley by motor convoy to sail from Southampton on the Liberty Ship S. S. James Woodrow.

10th January
- Arrival in LeHavre, France.

14th January
- Convoy departs for Central Air Depot Area Headquarters.

21st January
- Whole company with the exception of Detachments C, D, and F assigned to Fontenay, France, where it was necessary to renovate a furniture warehouse that had been used by the occupying German Forces to manufacture synthetic gasoline for the German war effort. This depot served the air bases on the Continent in the same way that Station 522 served the air bases in the U.K.

DETACHMENT C. - to remain at Marseilles.

DETACHMENT D. - to remain at Compeigne.

DETACHMENT F. - assigned to Compeigne to work alongside Detachment D.

June.
- Closure of base at Fontenay.